THE UNITED STATES AND PUERTO RICO

Decolonization Options And Prospects

ROLAND I. PERUSSE

Foreword By
GERALD R. FORD

THE UNITED STATES AND PUERTO RICO

Decolonization Options And Prospects

ROLAND I. PERUSSE

Foreword By
GERALD R. FORD

UNIVERSITY
PRESS OF
AMERICA

Lanham • New York • London

Copyright © 1987 by

University Press of America,® Inc.

4720 Boston Way
Lanham, MD 20706

3 Henrietta Street
London WC2E 8LU England

Printed in the United States of America

British Cataloging in Publication Information Available

Graphics by Publishing Resources, Inc.
Santurce, Puerto Rico

Library of Congress Cataloging-in-Publication Data

Perusse, Roland I.
The United States and Puerto Rico.

Bibliography: p.
Includes index.
1. United States—Relations—Puerto Rico.
2. Puerto Rico—Relations—United States.   3. Puerto
Rico—Politics and government—1952-
I. Title.
E183.8.P9P47   1987   303.4'8273'07295   87-21631
ISBN 0-8191-6657-X (alk. paper)
ISBN 0-8191-6658-8 (pbk. : alk. paper)

All University Press of America books are produced on acid-free
paper which exceeds the minimum standards set by the National
Historical Publication and Records Commission.

To Luz Amalia,

devoted wife, companion and helper

TABLE OF CONTENTS

FOREWORD

I have never ceased to admire the people of Puerto Rico. Through the dint of hard work, they accomplished an economic miracle, lifting their little island from the poorest to the most prosperous in the Caribbean in little more than a half century. They have contributed richly to American life. Thousands have served with honor in our armed forces. The latest of Puerto Rican heroes is Capt. Fernando L. Ribas-Dominicci who piloted the U.S. plane downed in the raid against terrorist camps in Libya last year. He and Capt. Paul L. Lorence of San Francisco, weapons systems officer on the same plane, made the supreme sacrifice in that operation, giving their lives in order that the rest of us might live in greater tranquility. These two men symbolize one of the most glorious moments of U.S.-Puerto Rican friendship and cooperation to achieve common objectives.

Puerto Ricans from the island and from the mainland have served our nation well in many walks of life. Among them are many reknown generals, admirals and ambassadors. They have distinguished themselves in music, literature and the arts. We in the United States should not judge Puerto Rico exclusively by the negative stereotypes often associated with its immigrant groups in our midst. As in the case of other immigrant groups throughout our history, it has been mainly the poorer classes with little education who have come to our shore seeking economic opportunity. Even so, many have surmounted heavy odds to rise to responsible positions in our society. Still, it is on the island, itself, that the economic miracle has taken place. Puerto Rico has one of the highest standards of living in all of Latin America. More of its students are in attendance at its universities, and its people live longer, than in the United States. One must visit Puerto Rico and see for oneself in order to comprehend the transition which has taken place.

For these and other reasons, I have always felt that it would be of the greatest benefit to both the people of the United States and the people of Puerto Rico if Puerto Rico were admitted as a state of the U.S. federal union. I proposed legislation to be introduced into the Congress of the United States to welcome the people of Puerto Rico into the U.S. family of states, if that be the desire of the people on the island. Some progress had been made in the past to provide the people of Puerto Rico with a greater degree of autonomy and self-government. But no steps had ever been taken to bring Puerto Rico into a position of full equality and dignity within the American nation. Thus, I proposed a series of steps, including a referendum on the island, by which the U.S. citizens of Puerto Rico could assure their rightful place as equals alongside the U.S. citizens of the 50 states.

Many persons have wondered why I took this initiative, since I was about to leave the White House and would no longer have the leverage of executive power with which to press for the bill's adoption. The answer is simple: because it was the right thing to do. Every President before me, beginning with President Eisenhower, had expressed himself with respect to Puerto Rico's future. I wanted to go on record with respect to my own feelings. I wanted to let the world know the direction I thought the future of Puerto Rico should take. If the proposed bill did not prosper, so be it. People would know my sentiments, and the proposed bill would serve as a model to the attainment of statehood at a future time, when an official request for this status would emanate from the people of Puerto Rico, as I am convinced it will one day.

Why do I think that it would serve the best interests of both the people of the United States and the people of Puerto Rico to have Puerto Rico become a state of the union?

There are many reasons, of which personal and national security is foremost. At a time of turbulence in the Caribbean, people in Puerto Rico would be assured that the United States would be committed to defend Puerto Rico to the same degree as any other state of the federal union. And Puerto Rico, itself, would provide a safe, secure and reliable base for the defense, not only of Puerto Rico but of the U.S. Virgin Islands, the southern flank of the United States, and our friends in the region who might need assistance. U.S. military forces in Puerto Rico help protect sea lanes through which oil and other strategic materials flow to Puerto Rico and the United States. Puerto Rico is playing a vital role in the President's Caribbean Basin Initiative. The continued availability of base facilities in Puerto Rico is best guaranteed under statehood. Continued territorial status or independence portend uncertainty in this respect.

Other benefits of Puerto Rican statehood are political. The admission of Puerto Rico as a state of the union would bring to a close a long chapter of U.S. colonialism and earn new respect for the United States in the Caribbean, Latin America and around the world. Every year brings new condemnations of the United States at the United Nations on the so-called Puerto Rican question. U.S. prestige in the world would be enhanced if colonial control of Puerto Rico would end before July 25, 1998, the 100th anniversary of the U.S. invasion of the island. For the first time, under statehood, U.S. citizens in Puerto Rico would enjoy the same rights as U.S. citizens in the 50 states.

Statehood would bring to an end nearly five centuries of uncertainty as to Puerto Rico's political future. Under statehood, U.S. Puerto Rican relations would be placed on a more orderly and predictable basis. Commonwealth status is a half-way house between statehood and independence and gives rise to many problems and uncertainties. Historically, the culmination of territorial status has been statehood. The realization that statehood is an irreversible step would ultimately bring Puerto Rican terrorism to a halt, not only in Puerto Rico but also on the U.S. mainland.

Puerto Rico can be an asset to U.S. relations with the Caribbean and Latin America. The addition of a Spanish-speaking state to the U.S. family of states would enrich our nation and facilitate our relations with Latin America. We find in Puerto Rico an almost inexhaustable reservoir of highly-trained professional, administrative, scientific and technical personnel who are familiar with the peoples and cultures of Latin America and who can be placed at the disposal of both business and government in the pursuit of joint interests in the region.

Statehood would bring real prosperity to Puerto Rico, as it has to every other U.S. territory admitted to the federal union. Tourism and investment would multiply, as was the case in Hawaii. Fewer Puerto Ricans would feel compelled to migrate to the United States in search of economic opportunity. With the issue of status behind them, the people of Puerto Rico would be free to apply their talents and energy to social and economic development.

For these and many other reasons, I feel that the destinies of Puerto Rico and the United States are intertwined and mutually supportive. Because of the high degree of local autonomy accorded to the states under our federal system, few changes would be perceptible in Puerto Rico in the transition from territory to statehood. The culture and language of the island would be respected. The changes that would occur would be for the better, for example, new pride in U.S. citizenship, new hopes and confidence in the future, and a new determination to make Puerto Rico a better place in which to live.

This book goes far in clarifying the Puerto Rican mystique for both U.S. and island readers. For the first time we get a true feeling of the innermost thoughts of Puerto Rican political leaders with respect to the future of the island, often in their own words. We are also given a realistic appraisal of the possibilities for the realization of their various aspirations, and a suggestion for breaking out of the present colonial dilemma. The book goes far in clearing the air of several myths surrounding the Puerto Rican reality and points the way toward freedom and a better life for the inhabitants of the last major colony under the U.S. flag.

Gerald R. Ford
Rancho Mirage, California

PREFACE

Interest in relations between the United States and Puerto Rico has intensified as a result of the arrest and trial of 16 pro-independence Puerto Rican terrorists (*Macheteros*) in Hartford, Connecticut, and the introduction into the U.S. Senate and House of Representatives of bi-partisan bills calling for a plebiscite on the political status of Puerto Rico. Status will also be a major issue in the U.S. presidential primaries and general state elections to be held on the island.

This book is a policy study which analyzes the major issues in contemporary relations between the United States and its last major colony, presents the views of key political actors for their solution, and evaluates the prospects for the acceptance of such recommendations by the U.S. Government.

The purpose of this book is to stimulate thought and action with respect to the future of U.S.-Puerto Rican relations. July 26, 1998 will mark the centennial of the U.S. invasion of Puerto Rico. It would be an embarrassment to the people and governments of both the United States and Puerto Rico if the present colonial relationship extended beyond the century mark. Because of the length of time it will take to arrive at any decision to modify the current relationship in any major way, as well as the time required to implement such a decision, it is not too soon to begin the decolonization process.

All major political leaders in Puerto Rico have expressed varying degrees of dissatisfaction with the present relationship, which has been condemned each year since 1978 by the United Nations Decolonization Committee. But they disagree fundamentally on how the relationship should be changed. Indeed, the division is so profound that position on status forms the basis of the island's political party system. One of the two principal parties seeks "culmination" of the present free association arrangement. The second principal party wants statehood. And a third party, small but vociferous, agitates for independence.

The book argues that free association is no longer a valid option for Puerto Rico and recommends that the U.S. Congress ask Puerto Rico to hold a plebiscite between the two classic formulas for decolonization, statehood and independence.

The author has tried to present, as honestly and fairly as possible, the desires, wishes and demands of the proponents of each status alternative, as reflected in party platforms and in oral and written statements of principal party leaders. These are footnoted to permit anyone to check their accuracy. But, of course, it is difficult in some cases to establish a position with precision. Also, positions are subject to change. The author apologizes in advance for any misinterpretation which may have occurred, and would be pleased to be advised on how the presentation of any party or individual position could be improved.

The discussion of the prospects for the realization of particular status changes, as these have been advanced by their principal proponents, will probably generate the most controversy. No one has developed a reliable crystal ball to predict the future. The possible reaction of the U.S. Government, especially the U.S. Congress, to any request for change is difficult to foretell. Congress, which controls U.S. territories, is notorious for not committing itself until it is absolutely necessary to do so. So no one can know with certainty how Congress and the Executive Branch would react to any petition for change until it is officially formulated, formally presented, thoroughly discussed and finally acted upon.

No one can know for sure, but it is possible to make some educated guesses. There is a long history of the handling of U.S. territories by the President and the Congress. There is a long string of precedents to guide us. With respect to the present, there exists an elaborate litany of presidential statements and remarks by Congressional leaders and other officials, as well as a long record of executive, legislative and judicial action. This gives us some basis for speculating as to how Congress and The White House might react to any future request for change if and when formally presented.

I do not expect that all analysts will agree with my conclusions. There is ample leeway for different interpretation. I would like to invite those who honestly feel that U.S. action would be otherwise, in general or in specific terms, to speak out. One of the principal purposes of this book is to encourage a dialog on status prospects, so that the people of Puerto Rico, who at some future time may be called upon to choose among status alternatives, will know as much as possible about the possible consequences of their choice.

Because it travels deep into areas of controversy and uncertainty, the book relies heavily on original source material and carries extensive footnotes. A sincere effort has been made to turn out a scientific study and not a propaganda tract. Each reader will be able to judge for himself the extent to which this objective has been achieved.

I want to express my deep appreciation to the Rockefeller Foundation for a generous grant which enabled me to complete a major portion of this work.

Roland I. Perusse
San Juan, Puerto Rico

Chapter I

AN UNEASY SYMBIOSIS

Puerto Rico's close political association with the United States began in 1898 when the island was wrested from Spain by military invasion during the Spanish-American War. After two years of military occupation, a U.S. civil government was formed, and Puerto Rico was ruled directly from Washington for the next half century. American citizenship was extended to the people of Puerto Rico in 1917, and in 1947, Puerto Ricans were allowed to elect their own governor. Otherwise, the United States held tight control of the island.

The present government of the Commonwealth of Puerto Rico was established in 1952 as a compromise between those political forces on the island agitating for independence and those who wanted Puerto Rico to become a state of the U.S. federal union. It was a clever arrangement to cope with the political and economic problems at the time. Puerto Rico would enjoy extensive local autonomy in permanent union with the United States. With the status debate set aside, the island could concentrate on social and economic development. The new government was dubbed "Commonwealth" in English and Estado Libre Asociado in Spanish.

The free association formula was designed as an interim measure that would postpone but not prejudice the ultimate decision with respect to the island's final political status. Social and economic development were deemed essential to the island's happiness and welfare regardless of specific changes the future might bring.

The relationship was troubled from the beginning. Nationalist elements refused to accept the compromise and used violence to express their discontent. Most notable was the 1950 attack on Blair House in Washington, where President Truman was in temporary residence. In 1954, Puerto Ricans sitting in the visitors' gallery of the U.S. House of Representatives opened fire on U.S. congressmen during a vote on the floor. La Fortaleza, the governor's mansion in San Juan, was also stormed.

In 1959, the Puerto Rican Resident Commissioner in Washington introduced a bill (Fernos-Murray) to provide greater autonomy to Puerto Rico, but he withdrew the project when it became obvious that Congress was not willing to act.

In 1962, President John F. Kennedy and Puerto Rican Governor Luis Muñoz Marín set up a joint commission to study all aspects of the Puerto Rican status question. One of its principal recommendations—a status plebiscite— was promptly implemented. Commonwealth status was confirmed with 60 percent of the vote. Statehood attracted 39 percent, and independence less than one percent.

Another commission recommendation— the formation of periodic joint ad hoc advisory groups to advise on possible future improvements in U.S.-Puerto Rican relations— was also implemented. The first was formed in 1970 to study the possibility of granting Puerto Ricans the right to vote for President and Vice President of the nation. The group recommended the vote and advised a plebiscite on the question as soon as possible. This plebiscite still has not been held.

The second ad hoc group was formed to study all aspects of the U.S.-Puerto Rican relationship, and it recommended greater autonomy for the island government in a number of areas. A bill to implement these recommendation (HB 11200 - Pact of Permanent Union) was introduced into Congress in 1975 but died in committee with the adjournment of Congress in 1976.

Discontent peaked in 1978 as the leaders of the island's three political parties, including the Governor of Puerto Rico, each representing a different status preference, testified before the United Nations Decolonization Committee. The committee called for the transfer of all political power to the people of Puerto Rico. In 1981 and 1982, the committee recommended that the UN General Assembly debate the status of Puerto Rico. Heroic diplomatic efforts by the United States were required to stave off this debate.

In sum, U.S.-Puerto Rican relations under the present free association agreement (Commonwealth) have been uneasy at best and at times troubled and turbulent. Economic prosperity in the 1950s and 1960s under Operation Bootstrap seemed to vindicate the experiment, despite political malaise. But the economic recession and stagflation in both the United States and Puerto Rico in the 1970s returned the status issue to center stage, where it remains today.

Legal-political-constitutional factors

Relations between the United States and Puerto Rico are based on Public Law 600 of the U.S. Congress,[1] the Puerto Rican Federal Relations Act authorized by Public Law 600, and pertinent provisions of the U.S. and Puerto Rican Constitutions.

Public Law 600 allowed the people of Puerto Rico to establish their own local government. It repealed those portions of the Jones Act of 1917 which dealt with the structure and organization of the government of Puerto Rico, so as to permit the island a greater degree of self-government and more control of public policy.

The portions of the Jones Act not repealed by Public Law 600 concern relations between Puerto Rico and the U.S. federal government. These provisions were not changed by Public Law 600. They continue in force under a new designation, the Puerto Rican Federal Relations Act. Its sections are not numbered consecutively. Their enumeration is that of those portions of the Jones Act not abrogated by Public Law 600, and serves to emphasize the fact that basic U.S.-Puerto Rican relations remain unchanged by the grant of local government to Puerto Rico.

The most significant portion of the U.S. Constitution bearing on U.S.-Puerto Rican relations is Article IV, Section 3, paragraph 2, which reads: "The Congress shall have the power to dispose of and make all needful rules and regulations respecting the territory or other property belonging to the United States."

The most significant provisions of the Constitution of the Commonwealth of Puerto Rico bearing on U.S.-Puerto Rican relations are (1) the preamble, which recognizes Puerto Rico as being "within our union with the United States of America;" (2) Article I, Section 1, which states that the political power of the Government of Puerto Rico shall be exercised "within terms of the compact agreed upon between the people of Puerto Rico and the United States of America;" and (3) Article VII, Section 3, which reads: "Any amendment or revision of this constitution shall be consistent with the resolution enacted by the Congress of the United States approving this constitution, with the applicable provisions of the Constitution of the United States, with the Puerto Rican Federal Relations Act, and with Public Law 600, 81st Congress, adopted in the nature of a compact."

These four documents form the legal-constitutional basis for contemporary U.S.-Puerto Rican relations, but they do little to help clarify the basic nature of that relationship. Fundamental questions persist as to the kind of relationship that was intended and actually exists, even as to the meaning of the terms, "Commonwealth," and "Estado Libre Asociado," as used, respectively, to designate in English and Spanish, the body politic of Puerto Rico.

The preamble of Public Law 600 states that "this Act is ...adopted in the nature of a compact." The law was accepted by the people of Puerto Rico in a referendum, and the constitution which resulted was approved by both the people of Puerto Rico and the Congress of the United States. This new Puerto Rican constitution approved by the U.S. Congress uses the language, "compact agreed upon by the people of Puerto Rico and the United States," and U.S. Public Law 447 of 1952 also states that Public Law 600 "was adopted as a compact with the people of Puerto Rico." Thus, it can be argued, the United States has recognized that a compact, in the full meaning of the word, has been consummated between the United States and Puerto Rico.

A compact is a mutually binding agreement legally unalterable except by mutual consent. In 1953, in speaking before the Fourth Committee of the United Nations General Assembly, Mrs. Frances Bolton, U.S. Special Representative to the United Nations, termed the Federal Relations Act "a compact of a bilateral

4

nature whose terms may be changed only by common consent."[2]

In practice, however, most U.S. Supreme Court decisions seem to support the contention that the U.S. Congress has the power, under the territorial clause of Article IV of the U.S. Constitution, to change the U.S.-Puerto Rican relationship on a unilateral basis any time it seems so disposed, even without consulting the Government of Puerto Rico.

For example, in 1984, over the protests of the Government of Puerto Rico, the U.S. Congress denied the island the revenues from an increase in the tax on Puerto Rican rum sold in the United States even though the Puerto Rico Federal Relations Act states clearly that "all taxes collected under the internal revenue law of the United States on articles produced in Puerto Rico and sold in the United States... shall be covered into the Treasury of Puerto Rico." The Government of Puerto Rico did not even bother to contest the U.S. action in federal court.

Certainly the present arrangement between the United States and Puerto Rico is not a compact in the sense of a treaty between two sovereign nations, for it was not handled as such by the U.S. Senate. It is clear that, in practice, the U.S. Government considers that Public Law 600 and the Puerto Rico Federal Relations Act are domestic laws of the United States.

With respect to the terms, "Commonwealth," and "Estado Libre Asociado," the Constitutional Convention of Puerto Rico in 1952 decided to give these terms equivalent meaning, since "translation of 'Commonwealth' into Spanish requires a combination of words to express the concept of 'state' and 'liberty' and 'association.'"[3]

But, of course, the two terms, as generally used, have much different meanings. In one sense "Commonwealth" refers to certain states of the U.S. federal union, for example, the Commonwealth of Massachusetts and the Commonwealth of Virginia. In another sense, "Commonwealth" is the designation used to identify the contemporary international organization comprised of former British colonies. Clearly, the designation of Puerto Rico as a Commonwealth implies neither. It constitutes a new meaning for the term. It is a word pleasing to both U.S. and Puerto Rican ears, but has contributed to misinterpretations of the relationship by both parties.

But neither is Puerto Rico a "Free Associated State" in the full meaning of this term. Puerto Rico is not free in the sense of being a sovereign state. It is a territory of the United States. It is associated with the United States, but how is subject to much debate. And it is a state only in the generic sense of an organized political community. It is neither a nation state nor a state of the United States.

Puerto Rico's associational relationship with the United States does not fulfill all of the conditions for free association as they are set forth in United Nations resolutions.[4] For example, not all U.S. constitutional guarantees extend to Puerto Rico; Puerto Rico does not participate on a basis of equality in modifications of the U.S. Constitution; and Puerto Rico can not modify its own constitution without U.S. approval. The U.S. Government deals with Puerto Rico under the U.S. Constitution as a "territory or other property belonging to the United States."

In summary, interpretations of the nature of the relationship range from that of sovereign co-equals on the one extreme to that of being war booty, property or a colony of the United States on the other extreme.

The inhabitants of Puerto Rico are U.S. citizens and, with few exceptions, share all the rights and privileges enjoyed by U.S. citizens in the 50 states. They are exempt from paying all but a very few federal taxes, such as Social Security. On the other hand, their representation in the U.S. Congress is limited to one Resident Commissioner who can express himself on the floor of the House and in committee, but has no vote except in the committees to which he is assigned.

Puerto Ricans are subject to U.S. military service under the same conditions as U.S. citizens on the mainland. By their own choice, Puerto Ricans vote in U.S. presidential primaries on the island and participate in the national conventions of the major U.S. political parties but do not vote in general elections for the selection of the Vice President and the President of the nation. The Government of Puerto Rico has never requested the presidential vote, even though public opinion polls show that two-thirds of the people on the island would wish to exercise that right. Puerto Rico has its own political parties, which are not branches of U.S. political parties but rather are founded on the basis of differing positions with respect to the political future of the island. The pro-statehood New Progressive Party is split in its allegiance between the U.S. Republican and Democratic Parties, whereas the pro-Commonwealth Popular Democratic Party has traditionally supported the Democratic Party.

As in the case of U.S. states, Puerto Rico has a dual legal and judicial system. Federal law applies to Puerto Rico unless Puerto Rico is specifically exempted. State law is adjudicated by state courts and federal law by federal courts. There have been frequent conflicts as to jurisdiction, especially in the areas of civil rights, environmental control and criminal investigation. The U.S. District Court of Puerto Rico covers the geographical area of Puerto Rico and comes under the First Circuit Court of Appeals in Boston. Public opinion polls show that the people of Puerto Rico have more confidence in the U.S. District Court in Puerto Rico than in their own island judicial system.

The United States controls the external affairs of Puerto Rico, including foreign trade, customs, immigration, treaty-making, foreign travel and participation in international organizations.

Puerto Rico is currently rendering support to the nation's Caribbean Basin Initiative through its program for establishing "twin plants" in nearby countries of the Caribbean. These are industrial enterprises in which the first stage of production is accomplished in a country where wages are low and labor is mostly unskilled, and the semi-finished product is sent to Puerto Rico, a an area with more advanced technology, for the final stages of production and distribution.

Puerto Rico has also intensified cultural and commercial relations with neighboring countries, with special emphasis on Costa Rica, Jamaica and the Dominican Republic, and has sought investments for Puerto Rico from European countries and Japan. One such initiative, the negotiation of a tax-sparing agreement with Japan in 1986, was undertaken with insufficient consultation with the U.S. Department of State and was rejected by Secretary of State George Shultz.

The Police of Puerto Rico has worked closely with the U.S. Immigration and Naturalization Service to try to stem the flow of illegal immigrants into Puerto Rico from the neighboring Dominican Republic. It is estimated that from 500 to 1,000

Dominicans enter Puerto Rico illegally each month. The number of undocumented aliens from the Dominican Republic living in Puerto Rico surreptitiously is estimated at 100,000.

At one point, the Immigration Service ran out of funds with which to send apprehended Dominicans to their home island and began issuing them special entry permits until additional money was made available. Word of this new policy reached the Dominican Republic, and the number of boats crossing the rough, 60-mile-wide Mona Passage which separates the two Antillian islands began to multiply. During Fiscal Year 1986, the INS in Puerto Rico spent $384 million on the repatriation of Dominicans to their homeland.

The cost of illegal passage from the Dominican Republic to Puerto Rico varies from $500 to $5,000, depending on services rendered. Many boats are overloaded and are swamped in the high seas. Many lives have been lost in the crossing.

If they make it to shore, the illegals must hide from police and find a means of subsistence. Many are forced by circumstances to work surreptitiously at substandard wages for long periods of time.

It is estimated that about 20,000 Dominican illegals in Puerto Rico will receive amnesty under recent changes in U.S. immigration laws.

Economic factors

Puerto Rico's economic progress during the last 50 years, from being the poorhouse of the Caribbean, as characterized by First Lady Eleanor Roosevelt, to one of the most prosperous countries of Latin America and the Caribbean, is due in large measure to the Common Market arrangement which has existed between Puerto Rico and the mainland since the beginning of this century but did not begin to bear fruit for Puerto Rico until the years following World War II.

The principal components of the U.S.-Puerto Rican Common Market have been (1) the abolition of all tariffs between Puerto Rico and the United States; (2) a common tariff towards other countries; (3) a common monetary system; and (4) the free movement of labor between Puerto Rico and the United States.

Since 1902, there has been unrestricted movement of goods and services between Puerto Rico and the mainland. Puerto Rico collects an excise tax on some goods entering from the United States, notably on automobiles and electrical appliances, and there is a federal excise tax on certain Puerto Rican products sold in the United States, notably rum. But these are in fact taxes, not tariffs, and the tax on rum has been remitted to the Puerto Rican treasury since the beginning of the century.[5] Almost three fourths of Puerto Rico's trade is with the United States. If Puerto Rico were a nation, it would be the 10th largest trading partner of the United States.

With few exceptions, goods entering Puerto Rico from other countries are taxed at the same rate as goods entering the 50 states. The duty in Puerto Rico is collected by the U.S. Customs Service and remitted to the Puerto Rican treasury. There is close cooperation between Puerto Rican and federal authorities to curb contraband trade and drug smuggling, but with no better results than in the United States. As in the United States, there is considerable pressure to raise tariffs to protect local industry.

Since 1900, when Puerto Ricans were required to exchange their pesos for U.S. dollars, Puerto Rico and the United States have been using the same currency. U.S. banking laws apply to Puerto Rico, and deposits in Puerto Rican banks are covered by the Federal Deposit Insurance Corporation.

Puerto Ricans have been free to migrate to the United States since 1917, when U.S. citizenship was acquired. There has been a net flow of about 1.5 million Puerto Ricans from Puerto Rico to the continent since that time, which amounts to about half of the current population. The unrestricted right to travel to and live in the United States has served as an escape valve for the unemployed in Puerto Rico. But when jobs are hard to find in the United States, as in the oil crisis years of 1972 and 1976, there is considerable net reverse migration. Also, the character of many immigrants has changed in recent years. For decades, those who left the island for the United States were almost all poor, unskilled, with little education. At the present time, Puerto Rico is experiencing a brain drain, as many skilled professionals are leaving the island for what they consider better conditions and opportunities in the United States.

9

The saying is, when the U.S. economy sneezes, Puerto Rico's economy catches cold. The U.S. economy sneezed in the 1970's and Puerto Rico's economy staggered. During the decade, U.S. investment in Puerto Rico shrank; hotels closed; and unemployment rose to 20 percent. The stagnation extended to the 1980's when unemployment hit a record 25 percent. Many U.S. companies have shut down their operations in Puerto Rico, and some have moved their plants to neighboring islands where labor costs are lower.

Puerto Rico chafes under a number of economic controls. Perhaps the most vexing is a trade restriction (which applies equally to coastal U.S. states but not with such adverse effect) which raises the cost of Puerto Rican products sold in the United States and U.S. products sold in Puerto Rico: the requirement of U.S. maritime law (Jones Act) that ships of U.S. construction and registry be used in sea commerce between the states, including shipping between Puerto Rico and the mainland.[6]

The Government of Puerto Rico points to the high cost of air freight as an alternative means of shipping; also, to the obvious fact that ground transportation is not an alternative in interstate commerce for an island, and has asked to be exempted from this provision of the law, thus enabling Puerto Rico (and mainland shippers) to use foreign vessels in U.S. commerce at considerable savings. A recent study has concluded that this measure has no justification, except perhaps in terms of national security interests.[7]

In 1984, the U.S. Congress made a concession with respect to the carrying of passengers by sea between the United States and Puerto Rico. The Puerto Rican Passenger Vessels Bill passed that year permits vessels of foreign registry (mainly cruise ships) to transport passengers between the United States and Puerto Rico, or to take on U.S. citizens in Puerto Rico, if no U.S. ship is available. Besides providing an alternative means of travel between Puerto Rico and the mainland, this exemption has been of some benefit to Puerto Rican tourism, and accordingly, to the Puerto Rican economy.

Though the United States generally permits Puerto Rico to set wages lower than the U.S. minimum, it has insisted on the application of the federal minimum wage to all local government workers in Puerto Rico. The salaries of government employees on the island have been notoriously low. Though this step has made government employees happy, it has strained the coffers of the Commonwealth and municipal treasuries.

Rulings of the U.S. Federal Trade Commission apply to the island, as do other agency rules and regulations, unless Puerto Rico is specifically exempted; however, there is no FTC office on the island. A tacit agreement is said to exist between U.S. and Puerto Rican authorities that no FTC rulings will apply to the island unless the Commonwealth Government specifically requests that they do. But in that case, the question of enforcement arises, since the Commonwealth Government is not authorized to enforce federal law and it is questionable whether a federal agency can delegate such power to a Commonwealth agency.[8]

Other economic areas in which the Government of Puerto Rico has requested greater autonomy include control of immigration (to protect jobs), communications (to take into account local norms), and environmental quality control (to adjust such regulations to development needs).

Individuals and corporations resident in Puerto Rico are exempt from the payment of all federal taxes except for social security withholding taxes. This exemption has been of great economic benefit to the island, and is the envy of U.S. taxpayers. However, the advantages of not having to pay federal taxes have been exaggerated. In the first place, since the people of Puerto Rico do not pay income taxes, they do not benefit from the federal government's program of revenue sharing. Secondly, since the income of Puerto Ricans is so much below the national average, few would be required to file an income tax form, and among those who would file, few would have to pay taxes or pay any significant amount.[9]

Under Section 936 of the U.S. Internal Revenue Code, U.S. corporations are granted full exemption from payment of federal taxes on profits from branch operations in Puerto Rico. This has served as an incentive to attract U.S. business to the island and was the foundation for "Operation Bootstrap," which resulted in spectacular economic progress in Puerto Rico in the 1950's and 60's. Thousands of new jobs were created, and funds deposited by these corporations in Puerto Rican banks accounted for about one-third of all monies available for investment on the island.

In addition, the Government of Puerto Rico has been allowed to levy a tollgate tax on these earnings as they are repatriated to the United States.

In 1985, Section 936 came under attack by the U.S. Treasury Department. With the automation of industrial plants in Puerto Rico, fewer jobs were being created. Light industries, such as electronics and pharmaceuticals, entered Puerto Rico mainly to take advantage of the tax exemption. 936 funds deposited in Puerto Rican banks were being used for consumer loans, rather than reinvestments that would improve the economy. Looking for additional revenues under the mandate of Gramm-Rudman-Hollings, the U.S. Treasury proposed the gradual elimination of Section 936 and its replacement with a tax credit based on the number of jobs created. Only the promise of the Government of Puerto Rico to use 936 funds deposited in Puerto Rican banks for the development of twin plants in the Caribbean under the Caribbean Basin Initiative saved Section 936. But the respite is temporary, pending Puerto Rico's ability to demonstrate that this idea can bring dividends to all concerned.

Puerto Rico also enjoys special exemptions under the Caribbean Basin Initiative. For example, if the Puerto Rican rum industry should be hurt by the free entry of rum from other parts of the Caribbean into the U.S. market, the United States is committed to off-set such losses by rebating to Puerto Rico revenue from excise taxes collected on the sale of such rums in the United States. Puerto Rico has also been given the authority, under the tax reform bill of 1986, to use funds deposited in Puerto Rican banks for the development of twin plants in the Caribbean.[10]

Puerto Rico benefits enormously from the transfer of federal funds to the island. In Fiscal Year 1986, such payments to Puerto Rico totaled $5.8 billion. Of this amount, 2.3 billion was assigned to the Commonwealth and its municipalities. This allocation accounted for nearly a quarter of the consolidated Government budget of that year. Another 2.4 billion went directly to individuals. Puerto Rico relies on federal funds for 30.% of its Gross National Product, compared with 11.6% for the average state.[11]

Forty-three percent of the population of Puerto Rico (413.000

families) receives nutritional aid, as compared with 10 percent in the United States. Since the program was instituted in Puerto Rico in 1974, the island has received about $8.6 billion in such aid. It was dispensed as food stamps, as in the United States, until 1982, using the same criteria for distribution. But, because income levels are so much lower in Puerto Rico than in the United States,[12] nearly 60 percent of the population was eligible for food assistance. In 1982, the U.S. Congress decided to render this kind of help through annual block grants of $825 million and authorized payment by check. This pleased recipients, but in the process one third of the funds previously received and some 250,000 needy were lopped from the program.

Federal assistance to Puerto Rico has been generous but nevertheless discriminatory. In nearly every program, U.S. citizens in Puerto Rico receive less than U.S. citizens in the United States, if U.S. standards are applied. On a per capita basis, federal expenditures in Puerto Rico are lower than those in any U.S. state ($1,786.36 as opposed to North Carolina, the next highest, which receives $2,398.84 and Alaska, the highest, which receives $4,857.77). The District of Columbia receives per capita federal aid of $21,745.87 a year. Although Puerto Rico has 1.3 percent of the nation's population, it receives only .7 percent of federal expenditures.[13]

Maximum monthly benefit per family under the nutritional aid program in Puerto Rico is $199. In the last year in which Puerto Rico received full benefits (1982), the maximum was $264. The family earning ceiling for receiving food aid in Puerto Rico is $8,000 per year; in the United States, families earning up to $14,000 a year can qualify.

Puerto Rico is completely excluded from the federal program of Supplementary Security Income, which benefits the aged, blind and disabled poor. This program would have a value of $466 million a year to Puerto Rico. Ceilings or limits are placed on three other human services programs: Medicaid, Aid to Families with Dependent Children; and Title XX of the Social Security Act, which consolidates social services assistance to the states into block grants.

Puerto Rico receives about $63 millions a year under Medicaid. The island would receive $310 million if it received full benefits. The average Medicaid payment per patient on the island is $21.50, compared to the U.S. average of $77.98.[14] A Puerto Rican pays as much as his U.S. counterpart to enter a hospital, even though hospital costs in Puerto Rico are lower, but the reimbursement in Puerto Rico is 50% less.[15]

The program of Aid to Families with Dependent Children gives a Puerto Rican family of four an average of $96.66 per month in benefits, of which $72.48 is the federal share. The same Puerto Rican family (or any other) living in New York receives $566.70 per month, of which $288.35 is the federal share.[16] The amount received by Puerto Rico under Title XX of the Social Security Act varies from year to year, but it is much less than the $314 a month received by the average U.S. family which qualifies for social security benefits.[17]

It is estimated that Puerto Rico is short-changed a total of $1.3 billion a year in federal programs.[18]

On the other side of the coin, it can be noted that an estimated $1.65 billion comes to Puerto Rico each year under the Social Security program, which is three times as much as Puerto Ricans pay in each year.[19] This places Puerto Rico 18th among the states of the union in terms of total receipts. Social Security payments, of course, are an earned right, based on earnings and withholding taxes paid.

If one applies U.S. criteria to the island, there is no question that Puerto Ricans, starting from a much lower economic base, are entitled to much more aid than they are getting. For example, in the award of Pell educational grants, nine out of 10 university students in Puerto Rico receive this aid, far above the national average. If some programs were not capped, they would double in size. But the basic question remains: should the poor be penalized because they are so poor and so numerous? Should needy American citizens living in Puerto Rico be treated with less compassion than needy American citizens living on the continent? The courts have sustained the right of Congress to accord different treatment to U.S. citizens in the territories, but Puerto Ricans view unequal treatment as a violation of their natural rights as U.S. citizens.

Socio-cultural and psychological factors

How can a people exercise political self-determination if they have not yet determined the nature of their collective self?

That, in a nutshell, is Puerto Rico's status dilemma.

Who am I? Where am I going? Where do I want to go? These are some of the questions at the root of Puerto Rico's identity crisis.

Puerto Rico lies at the confluence of the two principal cultures of the western hemisphere: Hispanic to the south and American to the north. Tourist brochures portray Puerto Rico as a happy blend between these two cultures. Were that it were so. In reality, two strong forces exert an inexorable pull on the soul of every Puerto Rican, like the poles of a magnet. He is caught betwixt and between. He does not know which way to go. The result is collective schizophrenia.

Differences in cultural orientation form the basis of Puerto Rico's political party system. The New Progressive Party identifies with the great democracy to the north. The Puerto Rican Independence Party identifies with Hispanic culture. The Popular Party claims to represent a compromise between the two. As a matter of fact, it too, is torn between its pro-US. and pro-Hispanic wings, with only a few willing to accept the best of both cultures.

Some anthropologists will say that Puerto Rico has developed its own, separate culture, an amalgam of many influences, not only Latin and Anglo-Saxon, but also Indian, African and European. They speak of a new and unique Puerto Rican culture, of Puertoricanism.

Perhaps so, and this has laid the ground for some fierce nationalism. Puerto Rico has many of the attributes of a nation. It has a homogeneous population, a well-defined territory, a shared historical past and a common language and is predominantly Catholic. Puerto Ricans consider themselves separate and distinct from other peoples and are so regarded by others. Though nominally U.S. citizens, they do not refer to themselves as Americans. This term is applied to those living in the United States. However, Puerto Ricans lack a common interpretation of their past and do not share the same aspirations for the future.

Manifestations of nationalism on the island have been strong, leading to deaths and assassinations in the name of *la patria*. In the realm of athletic competition, Puerto Rico has long had a separate sports identity. It participates in the International Olympics, the Pan American Games, and the Caribbean and Central American Games. Puerto Ricans speak about their national team, national flag, national hymn, national ballet, national bank, etc. In statistical charts, trade with the United States is listed as foreign trade.

Yet the dichotomy persists. A pro-statehood administration will adopt the tourist slogan, "Puerto Rico, U.S.A." and its publicity will give equal prominence to the U.S. and Puerto Rican flags. Then a pro-Commonwealth government takes over and drops "U.S.A." from the slogan. Not daring to exclude the American flag completely, it places it half-hidden behind the Puerto Rican flag.

Puerto Rico celebrates U.S. holidays, Hispanic holidays (mostly in honor of patron saints) and its own holidays. Christmas is balanced off by Three Kings Day. There are three national holidays, one to satisfy each status preference: The Fourth of July, to commemorate the birth of the American nation; Constitution Day, to commemorate the establishment of Commonwealth; and the *Grito de Lares*, to celebrate an abortive uprising against Spain in 1868.

Channel 6, the government-owned radio and television station, was established to promote Puerto Rico's cultural heritage. It plays the traditional musical of the *danza*, the *plena* and the *bomba*, while other stations provide a diverse fare which includes American rock, Latin American rhythms and Puerto Rico's own *salsa*.

In the department stores, traditional guayaberas hang on racks next to stylish suits and blue jeans.

A young Puerto Rican is caught between his love for his *paso fino* (a fine breed of horse peculiar to Puerto Rico) and the allure of a new Corvette sports car racing by, between rice and beans and a hamburger and french fries.

While it can be argued that all this makes for rich cultural pluralism, it also results in conflict and antagonism. The anti-American grafitti on the walls of Social Science and Humanities buildings at the University of Puerto Rico (sustained in large part by U.S. funds) vies with the worst in anti-U.S. propaganda encountered in communist countries.

Puerto Rico has two official languages, established by law in 1902, English and Spanish. But Spanish is the common language of the people, spoken in most homes, in public places, at work and in government. One significant exception is the U.S. District Court of Puerto Rico, which is required to use English in all of its proceedings. This is because it must forward its records in English in case of appeals to higher federal courts. Translations would delay this proceeding and represent additional expense. Simultaneous interpretation is provided in Spanish for those who wish it. Use of Spanish only in the conviction of a non-Spanish speaking U.S. citizen by a Commonwealth court was upheld by the First U.S. Court of Appeals in Boston in 1981.

Spanish is also the language of instruction in the public school and in most private schools and universities. A recent attempt by the government to force private schools to teach in Spanish was abandoned because of their strong resistance. English language textbooks predominate at the university level, mainly because of the relative efficiency of U.S. publishers. English is a required subject through the second year of college, but the quality of instruction, especially in public schools, leaves much to be desired. A proposal in 1986 to eliminate the teaching of English in the first three grades was withdrawn when it met with widespread popular opposition.

Puerto Rico has an English-language newspaper and English-language radio and television. Also, magazines and newspapers are flown in from the United States. English is used widely in business, commerce, banking and tourism, and knowledge of both English and Spanish is a requirement for most better paying jobs.

It is often claimed that Puerto Rico is a bilingual society, but the truth of this statement depends on one's definition of bilingual. Webster defines bilingual as "using or able to use two languages, especially with the fluency of a native speaker." Perhaps most of the people are able to use two languages to a degree. But those able to use both English and Spanish, each "with the fluency of a native speaker," are much fewer. And those able to read, write, speak and understand both languages equally well, shifting effortlessly from one to the other, and operating with equal effectiveness at a professional level in either tongue, are very few, perhaps no more than 10 percent of the population.

Puerto Ricans are a deeply religious people, with strong family ties which stretch out to the extended family. For most, there is no more pleasurable way to spend a Sunday afternoon than to visit relatives. The monument to the Puerto Rican *jibaro* (the common man of the interior) perched at the crest of the new San Juan-Ponce expressway, symbolizes the nostalgia and romance of a simple country life.

The basic values of Puerto Rican life are said to be love of freedom and democracy and deep pride and respect for human dignity. As an indication of the depth of feeling in this connection, the Constitution of Puerto Rico flatly prohibits any kind of wire tapping and guarantees absolute right of bail under any and all circumstances. Proposals by the Secretary of Justice to modify these two provisions to make it easier to combat the rampant crime on the island have met with stiff opposition. People are willing to risk their lives to guarantee their freedom and privacy.

Organizations run the gamut of Lions, Rotary, Kiwanis and the League of Women Voters on the one hand to the *Ateno* on the other, a literary club whose members generally favor independence for Puerto Rico. But signs of Americanization are everywhere. Fast food restaurants are replacing the traditional roadside Puerto Rican kiosk. The women's liberation movement is putting a damper on machismo. There is now widespread concern for proper diet, physical fitness and weight control. The counters of Moscoso pharmacies display a wide selection of contraceptives for purchase by any one of any age.

There is tight state control of education, public and private, at all levels. The Department of Education administers the public school system and sets standards for the private schools. A new plan of educational reform has been undertaken to place more emphasis on the island's history and heritage. The Council of Highter Education serves not only as the governing board of the state university system but also as the licensing and accrediting authority for private colleges and universities. The Middle States Association of Colleges and Schools is being squeezed out, which will make it harder for Puerto Rican students to transfer credit to and from the island.

But education outside the classroom is equally significant in molding Puerto Rican character. Cable TV from the United States is spreading throughout the island, contributing to both English learning and knowledge about U.S. life and culture. American motion pictures are everywhere, in theaters, video shops and on television, many dubbed in Spanish. Direct Distance Dialing makes it easier to communicate with a relative in New York than one at the other end of the island. There are a myriad of opportunities for contacts with Americans from the north, not only in San Juan but at tourist spots and industrial sites throughout the island.

Throughout its history, Puerto Rico has served as a refuge for those fleeing tyranny and revolution in Latin America. Old, established non-Hispanic sounding family names such as Ferré, Chardón, Cole, Martín and McConnie abound in the telephone directory and have long been accepted on the island as authentically Puerto Rican.

Recently, some xenophobia has set in with the influx of Cuban refugees into Puerto Rico. There is pressure in some quarters to control the entry of foreigners, and even of U.S. citizens from the mainland, if this could be done, on the grounds that there are not enough jobs in Puerto Rico for a continuously growing population. Actually, the number of Cubans and mainland Americans coming to live on the island are few in number. Because they are generally well-educated, hard-working and highly motivated, they usually establish businesses and create employment rather than take away jobs. Like the refugees of the past, they are making a significant contribution to the island's growth.

Migration of Puerto Ricans to and from the United States is continuous. According to the U.S. Bureau of the Census, there are about 2,562,000 first and second generation Puerto Ricans living in the United States. In some years, reverse migration to the island has exceeded outflow. But to produce a net of a few thousand either way, it is estimated that up to a million persons are in motion each year. Passengers on night flights seem to fall in two categories: happy faces going to weddings, baptisms or graduations and unhappy faces going to funerals. In either case,

19

thousands of Puerto Ricans move between the United States and Puerto Rico each year, bringing U.S. and Puerto Rican culture close together.

In past years, Puerto Rican emigrants to the United States were mostly unskilled persons with limited education seeking employment. This has changed in recent years. For the first time in its history, Puerto Rico is experiencing a brain drain to the mainland. Engineers, architects, doctors, nurses, teachers and policemen, among others, all in short supply in Puerto Rico, are moving to the United States for better living conditions and greater professional opportunities.[20]

Puerto Rico has its share of illegal immigrants, 150,000 by some estimates, most from the Dominican Republic. Others are citizens from poor English-speaking islands in the Eastern Caribbean. If the unfortunate soul can make it up the ladder of English-speaking islands of the Lesser Antilles to, let's say, Tortola, he or she is practically "home free." There is a heavy daily migration of workers between the British and U.S. Virgin Islands. Of course, the illegal may prefer to stay in the English-speaking U.S. Virgins. But if that person chooses to come to Puerto Rico, only the air fare, which can be earned quickly in illegal work, separates him from his destination.

The Institute of Puerto Rican Culture, state radio and television, the liberal arts faculties at the universities, among others, fight hard to conserve and perpetuate traditional Puerto Rican culture, but they may be waging a losing battle. Not even the tightest totalitarian dictatorship could shut out external influences from a nation so close and so powerful, with such a highly developed communications technology, and with which it shares a common market and a significant minority group.

Two recent developments, however, serve to reinforce the Hispanic dimension in Puerto Rican culture: (1) the conversion of Spain and many Latin American nations to democracies in the last few years, making them more acceptable, ideologically, to their Puerto Rican brethren; and (2) preparations for the celebration in 1992 of the 500th anniversary of the discovery of the New World by Christopher Columbus. The latter is rekindling interest in the 400 years of history which Puerto Rico shared with the mother country and the other former colonies of Spain in the hemisphere. Puerto Rican participation is being coordinated at the highest level of government.

But change is inevitable. The modern inevitably overtakes and overwhelms the past. It is only a question of time before majority sentiment evolves among the people of Puerto Rico either to cast their lot with the United States or with Latin America and the Caribbean.

Security factors.

The common defense arrangement between the United States and Puerto Rico obligates the United States to provide security and protection to the people of Puerto Rico in return for the cooperation of the people of Puerto Rico in this joint defense effort.

The United States is responsible for devising the appropriate strategy for joint defense, planning for all possible contingencies, maintaining effective military forces in the region, and assisting in the maintenance of internal security. The United States assumes all costs for common defense. Defense is not an item in Puerto Rico's budget. Thus, the island has been able to concentrate its limited resources on social and economic development, especially education, which accounts for approximately one third of Puerto Rico's budget.

Puerto Rico's principal contribution to the common defense is made in time of war. As U.S. citizens, young men in Puerto Rico are subject to compulsory military service in time of emergency, on the same basis as young men in the United States. In time of peace, Puerto Rican youth are accepted for volunteer service as are youth on the mainland.

An estimated 179,468 Puerto Ricans have participated in the four major U.S. wars of this century, of whom 2,285 died in combat.[21] On a per capita basis, there are more young people from Puerto Rico in the U.S. armed forces than from three-fourths of the states of the union.

The common defense arrangement has worked well throughout the twentieth century. The U.S. Navy was effective in keeping sea lanes clear for shipping to Puerto Rico in both World Wars. The all-Puerto Rican 65th Infantry Regiment distinguished itself for its heroism in World War II and in Korea. One of the two casualties in the U.S. raid on Libyan terrorist camps in 1986 was a Puerto Rican pilot. Americans in Puerto Rico have made as great a contribution to the defense of our nation in this century as Americans living on the continent.

The principal threat to Puerto Rico and the United States today comes from Communist Cuba and the Soviet Union. The commandant of the U.S. Naval Station at Roosevelt Roads in Puerto Rico has stated that the Soviet presence in the Caribbean has increased ten-fold in the past 12 years. A State Department White Paper reports that the Soviet Union has sent a total of 24 naval task forces to the Caribbean since 1969. The Soviets have 6,000 to 8,000 civilian advisors and technicians in Cuba and over 7,000 military personnel including a combat brigade.[22] Cuban and Soviet naval units hold joint maneuvers in the Caribbean on a regular basis.

The Soviets have built a submarine base at Cienfuegos, on the southern coast of Cuba, where Soviet nuclear-powered submarines are regularly serviced. These facilities are believed to include an area for handling nuclear warheads, and a rail link to Punta Movida, which is believed to have facilities for servicing nuclear weapons. The Soviet brigade in Cuba has had training in guarding and handling nuclear weapons.

The Soviet Union has provided over $5 billion in military aid to Cuba since the installation of Fidel Castro as head of the Cuban government.[23] In the past year alone, according to Castro, Cuba has tripled its armed strength. He has said that Cuba now has half a million regular and reserve troops and over a million persons in the territorial militia. He has the second largest military force in the hemisphere after the United States. Over 200,000 Cubans have had combat experience in Angola.

The authoritative reference book, Wyers Warships of the World, reports that Cuba has 200 jet fighter planes, four large and two small submarines, 30 nuclear capable missile boats, four guided missile frigates and six submarine chasers, among other craft. The Cuban airforce is the fifth largest in the world. It is larger than those of all the other Caribbean Basin countries combined. It is believed to include at least 35 MIG 27 fighter bombers, capable of reaching all of Florida, parts of Alabama and Georgia, and all of Puerto Rico.[24]

It has also been reported that Cuba has the capacity to transport up to 15,000 military personnel by sea or air to any part of the Caribbean. Many Cuban surface vessels and aircraft are capable of carrying nuclear weapons to both Puerto Rico and the United States and indeed, may be so armed. Cuba has not signed the Treaty for the Prohibition of Nuclear Arms in Latin America, popularly known as the Treaty of Tlatelolco.

The U.S. Naval Station at Roosevelt Roads, together with bases in Panamá and Guantánamo, Cuba, guard Caribbean approaches to Puerto Rico and the United States. U.S. treaties for the bases in Panamá and Guantánamo will expire at the end of the century. If these treaties are not renewed, Puerto Rico will be the sole bastion of the United States for defense of the Caribbean.

There are honest differences of opinion as to the strategic importance of Puerto Rico to global U.S. defense and the U.S. national interest. In an era of intercontinental missiles, space stations and virtually undetectable submarines, does a regional defense strategy make sense?

The Navy says it does. In fact, it considers the U.S. naval base at Roosevelt Roads, one of the world's largest, to be critical to U.S. defense. Without this facility, according to the Navy, it would be extremely difficult, if not impossible to guarantee the security of either Puerto Rico or the United States. The Roosevelt Roads-Vieques complex, for example, is said to be the only place under the U.S. flag where the United States can hold realistic amphibious military exercises in a tropical setting.

In an interview with journalists, Commodore Diego E. Hernández, commander of U.S. Naval Forces Caribbean, made the following assessment:

"A little over half of the oil that is imported to the States comes through the Caribbean. Or, it originates in the region - Trinidad, Venezuela, Mexico. A lot comes through the Panama Canal from the Alaska oil fields to eastern ports.

"From the other direction, Middle East and Africa oil enters the Caribbean to Gulf refineries...

"If nothing else, there is vital interest in securing our ability to support this oil flow. In time of war, that interest will multiply as we certainly will need more oil, not less...

"The Panamá Canal has 14,000 ships going through it annu-

23

ally. All of this affects the United States very importantly, because the bulk of the cargo going through is energy-related coal as well as oil. The second largest chunk is grain.

"62% of this cargo originates in U.S. ports, and 31% is going to U.S. ports. Twenty-eight percent of it is petroleum or petroleum products and 10 percent is coal and ore...

"Let's add 3.5 million Americans in Puerto Rico and the Virgin Islands and you have an idea of how important the protection of our interests in the Caribbean can be."[25]

Ramey Air Force Base on the northwest corner of Puerto Rico, once part of the Strategic Air Command, was deactivated in 1973 on condition that it can be reactivated at any time during an emergency. It has been converted to a civilian airport under custody of the Government of Puerto Rico but is used intermittently by military aircraft during exercises. The island of Vieques, two-thirds of which is federal land, is used in conjunction with Roosevelt Roads for targeting, maneuvers and other military exercises, many in conjunction with European, Latin American and Caribbean allies of the United States. From Roosevelt Roads and Guantánamo Bay, the U.S. Navy controls the three principal straits of the Caribbean: the Straits of Florida and the Windward and Mona passages. Puerto Rico served as a base for launching military operations in the Dominican Republic in 1965 and Grenada in 1983.

There has been a certain amount of opposition to U.S. military activities in Puerto Rico, most of it organized by pacifist, environmentalist or leftist groups, but probably no more than in the United States or any other free society. For ten years, opposition to U.S. Navy activity was strong on the off-shore island of Vieques. Fishermen claimed that constant Navy shelling destroyed their fishing grounds and means of livelihood. Independence-minded groups from Puerto Rico proper descended on the beleaguered island and organized anti-Navy protests and demonstrations, including attempts to ram Navy vessels.

At this point, the Navy assigned one of its most brilliant officers, a native-born Puerto Rican, Commodore Diego E. Hernández, to command the U.S. Naval Station at Roosevelt Roads. In cooperation with the people of Vieques, agencies of the U.S. and Puerto Rican governments and private enterprise groups,

Hernández reached an agreement for Navy use of Vieques which would respect the rights of the inhabitants and still allow the Navy to complete its mission there, and for a long-range economic development plan to spur economic growth on the island. New industries were brought in; new agricultural and marine projects were developed; and the Department of Defense awarded some attractive military contracts to the island. As a result, unemployment, which had reached 50% in 1982, was reduced to 30% by 1986 and was expected to reach zero within a few more years. Some of the best friends of the U.S. Navy today live on the island of Vieques, Puerto Rico.[26]

Another problem arose from the disclosure of a highly-classified Joint Chiefs of Staff document, the 1975 Nuclear Weapons Deployment plan, under terms of the Freedom of Information Act. This document was a detailed contingency plan for U.S. deployment of nuclear weapons in Bermuda, Canada, Iceland and Puerto Rico in case of national emergency.

The release of this information caused problems for the United States in all four localities, but in Puerto Rico, difficulties were compounded by the existence of the 1967 Treaty for the Prohibition of Nuclear Arms in Latin America (the Treaty of Tlatelolco). This treaty prohibits the receipt, storage, installation or possession of nuclear weapons by the signatory nations. The United States is not a signatory but agreed to a protocol of the treaty which explicitly bars the receipt, storage and deployment of nuclear weapons in Puerto Rico.

William N. Arkin, director of the Arms Race and Nuclear Weapons Research Project at the Institute for Policy Studies in Washington, D.C., received a copy of this report and promptly sent additional copies to "authorities" in all four countries. He wrote a major portion of a report on Puerto Rico for the Puerto Rican Bar Association, which released it on August 28, 1984. The report charged that the "nearly-constant presence of nuclear devices on U.S. ships and planes in Puerto Rican waters and air space is a violation by the United States of the Treaty of Tlatelolco."

The report caused hardly a ripple in Puerto Rico at the time. The Puerto Rico Bar Association is controlled by the left wing in Puerto Rican politics, and its reports are read in that light.

It was only when essentially the same information was published prominently on the front page of *The New York Times* February 13, 1985 that Puerto Rico took notice. A total of seven anti-nuclear groups and movements were eventually organized or took part in protests and demonstrations. The Speaker of the Puerto Rican House of Representatives was pressured into holding hearings. He rendered a report on March 24, 1987 to the effect that no nuclear weapons were stationed on Puerto Rican soil but that the infrastructure exists, so that when the United States so determines, it can use island territory for the storage, transportation and propulsion of nuclear devices. This, the report said, does not constitute a violation of the Treaty of Tlatelolco.

However, the report stated that "if the transit of ships with nuclear arms is so frequent as to constitute the equivalent of continuous presence of this type of armament on the island, this would not be a violation of the letter of the treaty, but it would of its spirit." The Department of Defense has stated that it does not believe it is a violation of the treaty to prepare a military base to receive nuclear weapons as long as the weapons themselves are not put on the base.

There are three paramilitary organizations in Puerto Rico: the U.S. Coast Guard, the Puerto Rican National Guard and the Reserve Officers Training Corps (ROTC).

The San Juan, Puerto Rico, Coast Guard is headquarters of the U.S. Coast Guard's Greater Antilles Section, which is responsible for Coast Guard operations in the Caribbean from the Dominican Republic to Surinam in South America. The Section has 465 active duty personnel and 55 civilian workers at bases in San Juan, Aguadilla, Ceiba and Ponce, in Puerto Rico, and at St. Croix and St. Thomas in the U.S. Virgin Islands. Their principal activities are search and rescue missions and law enforcement (principally the interception of drug smugglers). The number of vessels and the amount of drugs seized has steadily increased since 1981; nevertheless, it is estimated that up to three-fourths of such vessels escape detection.

Pressure on smugglers by law enforcement officials in the southeastern United States has caused them to shift their operations further to the east and to off-load further north in the United States. This has meant more work for the Greater Antilles Section.

At Aguadilla, Puerto Rico, the Coast Guard has four Dolphin helicopters and three Falcon jets.

Other Coast Guard duties include the operation of lighthouses; the installation of fixed and floating aids to navigation; inspection of passenger ferries, charter boats and pleasure craft; and pollution monitoring and control.[27]

The Puerto Rican National Guard, divided between the Air National Guard and the Army National Guard, and totaling some 11,750 members, has performed the usual domestic functions in emergency situations, such as flood aid and strike control. But it has also played a significant international role. The Guard has built roads in Panamá, repaired hurricane-damaged communications in the Dominican Republic, trained home guard units from several Caribbean countries, and participated in joint exercises and maneuvers with military and paramilitary units of several countries. Its dual language capacity gives it additional value in this respect.

In recent years contingents from the Puerto Rican National Guard have participated in Tall Pine and Minuteman exercises in Central America with guardsmen from several U.S. states. Marxist and independence advocates in Puerto Rico claim that this training is a prelude to sending the Puerto Rican National Guard into combat in Nicaragua.

Finally, it should be noted that the U.S. Air and Army Reserve Officers Training Corps (ROTC) offers classes at the University of Puerto Rico in Río Piedras and in Mayaguez. Because of the opposition to military training on campus by certain segments of the student body, training is administered at installations on the edge of the university. Students taking classes at nearby colleges and universities are also permitted to enroll. The ROTC offers a young Puerto Rican mobility in American society. He or she has a good chance of becoming an officer in the U.S. Army or Air Force through this program, administered in Puerto Rico. Chances would be less if that person enlisted and tried to compete for Officers Candidate School in the United States, because of different cultural background.

The police of Puerto Rico and the Federal Bureau of Investigation cooperate in the fight against organized crime in Puerto Rico. Since October 1982, according to F.B.I. statistics, 128 indictments, complaints and legal briefs have been filed against leaders of organized crime on the island. The result has been 93 convictions against ten acquittals. Among those indicted were 22 police officers and six attorneys.

Some of the police officers were responsible for the most heinous crimes imaginable: cold-blooded killings, kidnappings and murder-robberies. A master network of crime, directed from within the confines of the police headquarters, was exposed and broken up.[28]

In addition, 30 accusations of conspiracy to defraud the U.S. Government were filed under Operation Greenback, which has been investigating money-laundering in Puerto Rico since 1983.

The fight against the traffic of narcotics into and through Puerto Rico is led by a well-equipped intergovernmental task force called FURA (United Forces in Rapid Action). The Puerto Rican government agencies involved are the Police, the Ports Authority and the Air National Guard. The federal agencies include the Drug Enforcement Administration, the Federal Aviation Administration, the U.S. Coast Guard, the U.S. Customs Service and the Federal Communications Commission. In one month alone (November, 1986), the FURA task force intercepted cocaine and marijuana with a total street value of $1.39 billion.[29]

FURA has been the subject of study of many U.S. state, county and municipal governments and has served as a model for similar systems of interdiction in other parts of the nation.[30]

One of the most dramatic examples of cooperation between U.S. and Puerto Rican government agencies to fight crime occurred in relation to the arson fire at the Dupont Plaza Hotel in San Juan December 31, 1986. Police, National Guard and Navy helicopters evacuated scores of guests from the hotel rooftop. The 30-man National Response Team of the U.S. Treasury Department arrived on the scene with modern equipment on New Year's Day and did not leave until they had determined the cause of the fire and how it spread. The Federal Bureau of Investigation worked with the Department of Justice of Puerto Rico in identifying those responsible, and federal agencies helped in the identification of all but one of the 97 victims.

Puerto Rico has not been immune to either domestic or international terrorism, and terrorism in Puerto Rico has spilled over to the mainland. Indeed, William Webster, then Director of the F.B.I., warned in testimony before the U.S. Congress March 4, 1987 that Puerto Rico could become the Achilles Heel of the United States. Ten of the 17 terrorist incidents which took place in the United States in 1986 took place in Puerto Rico, he said. The problem, he claimed, is partially political.[31] Frustrated by their inability to attract electoral support, extremist pro-independence groups have resorted to violence in an attempt to promote their cause. The results have usually been counterproductive, but the fanaticism continues.

Prior to 1979, incidents of terrorism in Puerto Rico were few, ill-planned and rather ineffective. They consisted of sporadic pipe-bombings, occasional sniping and other low-risk operations. Targets were usually U.S. recruiting stations, U.S. military bases and U.S. businesses. Damage was minimal, and loss of life was avoided.

This changed at the end of 1979 with the ambush of a U.S. Navy bus transporting personnel of the Sabana Seca Security Group. Two men were killed and eight were wounded. Three different groups claimed responsibility: Volunteers for the Puerto Rican Revolution, the Boricua Popular Army (*Macheteros*), and the Armed Forces of the People's Resistance. The assault was planned and executed with military precision.

Four months later, terrorists opened fire on a car transporting Army ROTC instructors to a class at the University of Puerto Rico campus in Río Piedras. There were no casualties, although one man received treatment for cuts from flying glass.

Another incident occurred at Fort Allen on the southern part of the island with the discovery of a sophisticated anti-personnel device in 1980. Whereas earlier explosives had been designed principally to cause property damage, the Fort Allen bomb was designed to cause casualties.

By 1980, two clandestine independence organizations were most feared: the *Macheteros* and the Armed Forces for National Liberation (FALN). The first was based in Puerto Rico, the second in the United States.

The most serious incident was the destruction by the *Macheteros* of nine National Guard fighter planes, and the damaging of two others, at the Muñoz Marín Air Base in San

Juan in January 1981. The resultant damage, $45 million, was the most extensive loss through terrorism in U.S. history. The assault was a carefully coordinated military operation which required considerable advance planning and technical knowledge.

On November 27, 1981, the *Macheteros* blew up two electric substations, leaving the Condado tourist area without electrical energy. The same day a lesser known group, the Liberation Movement, fired on and lightly wounded a guard at the Fort Buchanan entrance. On April 21, 1981, the *Macheteros* robbed an armored car of $348,000, and on June 29, 1981, the Organization of Volunteers for the Puerto Rican Revolution planted bombs at a bank on the south side of the island.

It was almost impossible for the police of Puerto Rico or the F.B.I. to penetrate the FALN or the *Macheteros*. They were organized into small cells of just a few members each. A member of one cell rarely knew the members of another, although certain individuals were members of more than one cell. Recruitment was carried out with great care, and safe houses were established where members lay low after an operation. The location of safe houses changed frequently.

In 1984, the F.B.I. termed the FALN the most dangerous terrorist group in the United States. It has been responsible for over 150 attacks since its organization in 1973. These caused six deaths and over $3.5 million in property damage.

The FALN was under surveillance in New York for seven years before the F.B.I. was able to make an arrest. The opportunity arose unexpectedly as a result of an accidental explosion at a bomb factory in Queens, New York. William Morales was taken into custody, tried and sentenced to 89 years in prison. A few months later 11 other members of the organization were picked up in Chicago. Despite having lost one eye and nearly all the fingers of both hands, Morales escaped by using 10 feet of elastic bandage to lower himself from a hospital window, and jumping the last 30 feet. He made his way to Mexico, where he was captured in a shoot-out with the Mexican police. He is in a Mexican jail, serving a 12-year prison term, and the United States has asked for his extradition.

The first real break in the long F.B.I. investigation of the *Macheteros* came on April 4, 1984 when a Puerto Rican police officer, summoned to investigate a series of petty burglaries, stumbled onto a *Machetero* hide-away in Puerta de Tierra, San Juan. Among the many items of incriminating evidence found at the scene was a list of names of over 100 *Macheteros* with their code names, addresses and telephone numbers.

Shortly thereafter, *Machetero* Carlos Rodríguez Rodríguez was picked up on charges of bank fraud and drug traffic. Later, he was additionally charged with the 1982 murder of a U.S. sailor and received a 57-year jail sentence.

On September 12, 1983, the second largest cash robbery in U.S. history occurred at West Hartford, Connecticut, where $7 million was stolen from a Wells Fargo armored car by a guard identified as Víctor Gerena. He disappeared from sight in what appeared to be the perfect crime. In October 1984, the *Machetero* organization announced to the world that Gerena was a *Machetero* and that the robbery had been committed in the name of the *Macheteros*. Gerena confirmed this in letters to the *Hartford Courant* and *El Mundo* newspaper in San Juan.

Another startling development took place in West Hartford on Three Kings Day, January 6, 1985, when *Macheteros* disguised as the three kings gave out gifts and money to poor children in a Puerto Rican neighborhood. One of the gifts, and a $20 bill, was placed in the hands of an F.B.I. agent who had the group under surveillance.

This was followed January 26, 1985 by a bazooka attack against the U.S. District Court in Old San Juan for which the *Macheteros* took responsibility.

Decisive action was taken by the F.B.I. on August 30, 1985. Twelve *Macheteros* were arrested in coordinated early morning raids in the Greater San Juan area. The twelve, together with another arrested in Dallas, Texas, and still another in Boston, Massachusetts, were charged with complicity in the Wells Fargo robbery. It was revealed by Department of Justice Secretary Edwin Meese that Gerena and some $4.5 million of the loot were believed to be in Cuba, and the rest in Puerto Rico.

Additional information was revealed in the bail hearings. The F.B.I.'s star accuser was none other than Carlos Rodríguez Rodríguez, who was given immunity for turning informer. At the time of the arrests, the *Macheteros* had already split into two groups, the Volunteers for the Puerto Rican Revolution, a political arm under the direction of Juan Enrique Segarra, that advocated less violent actions, such as the Three Kings giveaway, and the Boricua Popular Army or *Macheteros*, a military arm led by Filiberto Ojeda Ríos, identified as a Cuban agent, who recommended more violent action, such as the bazooka attack against the Federal Court. Segarra and Ojeda were said to have assisted Gerena in the Wells Fargo theft and to have been involved in the destruction of the nine National Guard jets in 1981.

All but two of the accused *Macheteros* are out on bail, awaiting the start of their trial. The evidence to be presented by the Department of Justice is expected to expose additional Cuban involvement with both the *Macheteros* and the FALN. As a final word on Puerto Rican terrorism, it should be noted that acts of political violence have been widely condemned by leaders of all three of Puerto Rico's principal parties and the public at large.[32]

NOTES

Chapter I

1. Puerto Rican Commonwealth Act, 64 Stat. 319, July 3, 1950

2. Frances Bolton and James F. Richards, *Report on the Eighth Session of the General Assembly of the United Nations*, 83rd Congress, 2d Session, p. 241.

3. Resolution 22, approved by the Constitutional Convention of Puerto Rico, in plenary session, February 4, 1952.

4. See criteria for free association established by United Nations Resolutions 742 (VIII) 1953 and 1541 (XV) 1960.

5. In 1984, Congress for the first time failed to authorize the remittance to Puerto Rico of a $2-a-gallon rise in the tax on Puerto Rican rum sold in the United States. Though there was talk among some Puerto Rican officials of challenging this violation of the Federal Relations Act in the federal courts, no action was taken.

6. Section 27 of the U.S. Merchant Marine Act of 1920, known as the Jones Act, not to be confused with the Jones Act of 1917.

7. Whitehurst, Clinton H., Jr. *American Domestic Shipping in American Ships: Jones Act Costs, Benefits and Options*. American Enterprise Institute, Washington, D.C., 1985

8. p. 15, *The San Juan Star*, October 17, 1983.

9. See the book, *Statehood is for the Poor*, by Carlos Romero Barceló, San Juan, Puerto Rico, 1985.

10. Twin plants is the popular terminology for complementary production in which the first stage, usually rudimentary, is performed in a country of low-cost labor, while the second, more sophisticated stage is performed in a country with high technology. Under this concept, unfinished Caribbean products enter Puerto Rico (and thus, the U.S. market) duty-free as long as the value added in Puerto Rico is at least 35 percent.

11. p. 18, *The Wall Street Journal*, October 30, 1984.

12. According to the Bureau of the Census, the median family income in Puerto Rico is $5,923. The U.S. median is $19,917. Mississippi, the state ranking last, has a median family income of $14,591. In Puerto Rico, 61.4% of the people fall below the U.S. poverty line.

13. U.S. Census Bureau.

14. p. 10, *The San Juan Star*, October 3, 1984.

15. p. 17, *El Mundo*, January 31, 1986.

16. p. 30, *The San Juan Star*, May 8, 1984.

17. *Ibid*.

18. p. 8A, *El Mundo*, February 8, 1983.

19. Interview with Earl Fernando Brady, District Manager, Social Security Administration, San Juan Office, February 1985.

20. p. 12, *El Nuevo Día*, April 20, 1986, and p. 20, The *San Juan Star*, December 1, 1982.

21. p. 5A, *El Mundo*, March 5, 1983.

22. p. 119, *Soviet Military Power 1985,* U.S. Government Printing Office, Washington, D.C. 1985.

23. *Ibid*.

24. *Op. Cit. Soviet Military Power, 1985,* p. 120.

25. p. B-5, *The San Juan Star* and p. 1 and 20, *El Nuevo Día*, May 15, 1983.

26. p. 48, *El Nuevo Día*, April 6, 1986; p. 48 *El Mundo*, April 26, 1986; testimony of Mary Ann T. Knauss, Deputy Assistant for International Affairs, U.S. Department of Commerce, before the Committee on Interior and Insular Affairs of the U.S. House of Representatives, May 20, 1986.

27. This section on the U.S. Coast Guard is based on an article in *The San Juan Star*, p. 5, Outlook Section, March 10, 1985, updated in 1986.

28. p. 25, *The San Juan Star*, September 26, 1986.

29. p. 4, *El Nuevo Día*, December 7, 1986 and p. 2, *The San Juan Star*, December 9, 1986.

30. p. 17, *El Mundo*, February 2, 1987.

31. EFE dispatch from Washington, D.C. which appeared on page 6 of *El Mundo*, March 5, 1987.

32. This section on Puerto Rican terrorism is based mainly on a review of coverage of such events over a period of years by the three principal San Juan newspapers: *The San Juan Star*, *El Nuevo Día* and *El Mundo*.

Chapter II

THE FREE ASSOCIATION OPTION AND ITS PROSPECTS

The present free association agreement between the United States and Puerto Rico, called Commonwealth in English and *Estado Libre Asociado* (Free Associated State) in Spanish, was established in 1952 by the Popular Democratic Party (PDP) of Puerto Rico under the charismatic leadership of Governor Luis Muñoz Marín.

Proponents of the continuation of Commonwealth view statehood and independence as extremes that divide the Puerto Rican people. They see the Free Associated State as a compromise which embodies many of the benefits of statehood without the dangers of political and cultural assimilation, and many of the benefits of independence (for example, a high degree of local autonomy) without the loss of the economic and military security afforded by close association with the United States.

Commonwealth advocates admit that the relationship can and should be improved, on the basis of past experience and changed conditions, but most *Populares* seek change within the range of the free association formula rather than by shifting to statehood or independence. Areas in which the party has sought a greater degree of autonomy include control of immigration, commerce, communications, environment, labor affairs and international relations.

The PDP takes the position that Commonwealth is a bilateral

compact between the United States and Puerto Rico that can only be changed by mutual consent.

In the past, the Popular Democratic Party has sought to "culminate" Commonwealth by securing additional powers for the island government. It has sought more flexibility in the application of U.S. laws and regulations, greater authority in some areas under federal control, greater voice in federal legislation affecting the island, exemptions from federal laws unless Puerto Rico is specifically included (and if included, the right to object and to have such objections acted upon by Congress), and the authority to participate in international organizations and to make treaties with foreign countries.[1]

Within seven years of the establishment of the Free Associated State, changes were sought, unsuccessfully, through the Fernos-Murray Bill of the 1950's (H.R. 5926 of March 23, 1959). The party spent four years during Rafael Hernández Colón's first term as governor (1972-1976) in another fruitless search for greater autonomy, which culminated in HB 11200 of August 1976. This bill was before the U.S. House Insular and Territorial Affairs subcommittee for two years, during which time it was extensively amended but never reported out.

During the late 1970's, while out of power, Hernández Colón prepared a basic policy paper, the New Thesis, calling once more for certain changes in political status. It served as a guide for his 1980 gubernatorial campaign, but when he lost, the document was set aside. However, the Popular Democratic Party won control of both houses of the legislature that year. Its most significant action bearing on U.S.-Puerto Rican relations was House Joint Resolution 22 of March 21, 1982, which listed 15 demands from the U.S. Congress:

1. Power to impose tariffs and other controls on goods entering Puerto Rico.
2. Power to make commercial agreements with other countries.
3. Power to control imports from the United States in order to protect local agricultural production.
4. Modification of U.S. maritime law to permit the use of foreign vessels in commerce between the United States and Puerto Rico.

5. The use of block grants for the assignment of federal aid to Puerto Rico.
6. Aid to Puerto Rican tourism by (a) eliminating the 24-hour restriction on the length of stay of cruise ship passengers in Puerto Rican ports; (b) permitting the use of foreign cruise ships between U.S. and Puerto Rican ports; and (c) eliminating U.S. taxes on items purchased by tourists in Puerto Rico.
7. Liberalization of Section 936 of the U.S. Internal Revenue Code which gives 100% federal tax exemption to U.S. firms investing in Puerto Rico.
8. The exclusion of rum from free entry into the United States under President Reagan's Caribbean Basin Initiative.
9. Likewise, the exclusion under the Caribbean Basin Initiative, of free entry into the United States for tuna, pineapple, electrical and electronic goods and other products important to the Puerto Rican economy.
10. Expansion of air routes between San Juan and foreign countries.
11. Establishment in Puerto Rico of centers for vocational and higher education, and commercial and professional training, for the purpose of assisting Caribbean countries.
12. Aid to specific agricultural products, for example, sugar cane, and energy production.
13. A separate quota for Puerto Rico on beef imports.
14. Elimination of textiles and clothing from Caribbean products given free entry into the United States under the Caribbean Basin Initiative.
15. Inclusion of Puerto Rico in programs of federal purchasing, and location and expansion of federal installations.

These 15 points were presented to the U.S. Congress in testimony by Representative Severo Colberg and Senator Sergio Peña Clos of the Puerto Rican Legislature. Limited measures were taken by Congress to meet Puerto Rico's demands with respect to tourism, Section 936 of the Internal Revenue Code and the Caribbean Basin Initiative (points 6, 7, 8, 9, and 11).

With respect to U.S. politics, the Popular Democratic Party participated in the 1980 U.S. presidential primary in Puerto Rico, backing Senator Ted Kennedy for the nomination. PDP leaders have always been close to the Kennedy family and consider the liberal wing of the Democratic Party as most friendly to the Commonwealth cause. That same year, Democrats in the New Progressive Party backed Jimmy Carter.

The PDP was again prepared to back Ted Kennedy for the 1984 nomination until he withdrew from contention. After some vacillation, the party decided not to endorse any Democratic candidate and left it to the individual judgment of each PDP member whether to work for a candidate of his or her choice, or even whether to vote at all.

In the meantime, the Democrats in the New Progressive Party decided to back Walter Mondale, who won the primary and Puerto Rico's 53 delegates.

Claiming that the Democratic primary was dominated by statehooders, a small group of PDP Democrats organized a caucus, which chose a rival slate of 53 delegates pledged to Senator Gary Hart. They unsuccessfully challenged the NPP Democrats, who voted as a bloc for Walter Mondale at the convention.

The PDP is badly split on the question of participation in U.S. politics. Some party leaders view U.S. politics as the politics of another country that has little or no relevance to Puerto Rico. Others see such participation as a means to gain leverage with The White House and the Congress. In any event, gone are the days when San Juan Mayor Felicia Rincón de Gautier hit the campaign trail for Hubert Humphrey in the United States, turning out thousands of Puerto Rican votes in his favor.

The party is also sharply divided on exactly what changes should be made in the present free association status, on the degree of intimacy that should exist in U.S.-Puerto Rican relations, and as to whether Commonwealth status should be regarded as permanent or transitory to either statehood or independence.

Because the party was split on status change, the 1984 party platform merely called for improvements in the Commonwealth relationship (without identifying them) while emphasizing that no fundamental change in status would be proposed in the 1984-1988 quadrennium. Instead, the party said it would concentrate on solving the social and economic problems of Puerto Rico, for example, crime, unemployment, housing, education, medical care and corruption in government.[2]

The Popular Democratic Party won the governorship and control of both houses of the legislature in 1984. Because of strict party discipline on voting, the party is in a position to stave off all proposals for changes in relations with the United States which run counter to the party's ideology and promote those which advance its ideology. For example, in 1983 the House and Senate passed a joint resolution (RC 1233) favoring Puerto Rican associate membership in UNESCO.[3]

In 1985, the Popular Democratic Party administration took strong initiatives in the field of international relations. Island leaders toured the Caribbean Basin countries, were received as foreign dignitaries (including 21-gun salutes for the Governor) and addressed national parliaments. According to Secretary of State Hector Luis Acevedo, the island was treated by host governments as a Latin American nation with special ties to the United States.[4]

Some of the activities brought the Puerto Rican Government in serious conflict with the United States. Chief of these were a commercial and cultural agreement with the Government of Costa Rica, which in effect would have established a Puerto Rican consular office in San José, and a tax-sparing agreement under negotiation with Japan, which ran counter to policies of the U.S. Treasury.

In practice, the pledge of the Popular Democratic Party not to seek changes in Puerto Rico's status has been interpreted as not seeking constitutional changes from Congress through the introduction of legislation, as was done in the past, but rather to acquire additional powers simply by exercising them.[5]

The policy of silence of the Popular Democratic Party with respect to political status was the result of a basic split within the party between "Old Guard" followers of the "father" of Commonwealth, Luis Muñoz Marín, who want to maintain close permanent union with the United States, and younger "autonomists" who want to loosen these ties. There are few Muñozistas in high position in the Puerto Rican government today. It is the autonomist wing of the party that has most influence on current Government policy.[6]

Since there exists no official Popular Democratic Party position with respect to the "culmination" of Commonwealth, it is necessary to examine the position of the more influential PDP leaders in order to get some idea of prevailing ideas within the party with respect to free association options.

The section which follows examines the views of Governor Rafael Hernández Colón, president of the Popular Democratic Party. Though hardly a *Muñozista*, he has tried to adopt a middle ground between the *Muñozistas* and the autonomists. This is followed by an examination of the position of Severo Colberg, former speaker of the House and leading apostle of the autonomists. Finally, the views of other ranking *Populares* are examined to see how close they come to the views of either Hernández Colón, Severo Colberg or both.

Position of Rafael Hernández Colón

The perception of Governor Rafael Hernández Colón of U.S.-Puerto Rican relations has gone through four four-year stages:

1972-1976. During his first term as Governor, an effort to attain greater autonomy for the island through negotiations with Congress;

1976-1980. Failing in this effort, and losing the governorship in the 1976 elections, four years of planning, culminating in his "New Thesis," with a view toward regaining the governorship and renewing his 1972-76 efforts to gain more autonomy from Congress.

1980-1984. Failing to regain the governorship by a narrow margin, four years "in the wilderness," years of uncertainty, self-examination and rethinking, culminating with the decision not to discuss status during the 1984 campaign nor in the 1984-88 quadrennium, should he be re-elected governor.

1985 and after. After regaining the governorship, an aggressive policy of acquiring powers and autonomy previously denied him, not through renewal of negotiations with Congress, but rather through quiet, piecemeal assumption of such powers until and unless the national government objects and takes action to stop him.

The inspiration for Hernández Colón's first four years in office came from the Pronouncement of Aguas Buenas on the Political Status of Puerto Rico, approved by the Central Committee of the Popular Democratic Party on November 18, 1970.[7]

In this pronouncement, largely the product of the more radical wing of the party, the Popular Democratic Party

1. proposed the convocation of a Constitutional Convention to formulate new terms for relations with the United States;
2. rejected outright the options of statehood and independence for the island;
3. endorsed "autonomy," that is, complete self-government, based on free association with the United States;
4. reaffirmed unconditional faith in Commonwealth status;
5. advocated clarification of the concept of common defense;
6. opposed exclusion of Puerto Rico from the Treaty for the Prohibition of Nuclear Arms in Latin America (Treaty of Tlatelolco);
7. requested jurisdiction over the entry of foreigners to the island;
8. declared the need to redefine the areas of strict local jurisdiction, distinguishing them from others in which jurisdiction may be exercised in consultation between Puerto Rico and the United States; and
9. demanded a thorough study of the compact between the United States and Puerto Rico to establish more precision with respect to compulsory military service, maritime commerce, customs, internal revenue, labor-management relations, air and maritime transportation, and communications (radio and television).

The pronouncement called for the maintenance of the "cultural personality" of the people of Puerto Rico. It asserted that the manner and mode of Puerto Rico's contribution to the common defense, including compulsory military service, should be the result of previous agreement between the two countries. In the meantime, the party would insist on the immediate withdrawal of the U.S. Navy from Culebra and Vieques, two islands off the east coast of Puerto Rico.

One of Hernández Colón's first acts in his first term was to form, in cooperation with President Nixon, an Ad Hoc Committee for the Development of the Free Associated State of Puerto Rico. Fourteen members were named, seven from the United States and seven from Puerto Rico, with former Puerto Rican Governor Luis Muñoz Marín and U.S. senator Marlow Cook of Kentucky as co-chairmen.

In his testimony before this committee, Governor Hernández Colón rejected both statehood and independence and called for continuance of permanent union with the United States with greater autonomy. He asked for greater jurisdiction in the area of environmental control, communications, sanitary regulations, use of insecticides, occupational health and safety, labor relations, immigration, maritime transportation, and foreign commerce and tariffs, along the lines of the Pronouncement. He asked the committee to consider the need for common agreement between the United States and Puerto Rico before federal laws were made applicable to Puerto Rico. Also, he requested that the committee consider delegating to Puerto Rico the responsibility for administering federal regulations in conformity with local conditions. He called for the assignment of federal aid to Puerto Rico in the form of a block grant, and for more latitude in the field of foreign relations.[8]

Hernández Colón set forth his plans in the international field in lectures at Yale University April 2-4, 1974:

1. to revamp and revitalize the concept of the democratic left in the Caribbean;
2. entry into the Caribbean Development Bank; and
3. participation in international organizations such as UNESCO, WHO, ILO and UNCTAD.[9]

The Ad Hoc Committee's recommendations were embodied in H.B. 11200, 94th Congress, lst Session, December 17, 1975, commonly referred to as the Compact of Permanent Union between Puerto Rico and the United States, or simply, "The New Pact."

On the surface, it appears that HB 11200 would have authorized considerably more autonomy to Puerto Rico in the areas that additional powers had been requested. However, close examination of the bill shows that the exercise of each proposed concession was conditioned on U.S. approval. In this sense, H.B. 11200 did not in fact grant any significant amount of additional autonomy to Puerto Rico than was granted under the Federal Relations Act it was meant to replace. In fact, H.B. 11200 demonstrated how *little* additional power the United States was prepared to give to Puerto Rico. Indeed, the only tangible gain would have been a Resident Commissioner in the U.S. Senate to match the one in the House. Extensively amended, H.B. 11200 died in the U.S. House Interior and Insular Affairs subcommittee with the expiration of the 94th Congress.

One additional observation should be made with respect to Governor Hernández Colón's position on status during his first term.

In an interview with a reporter from *The San Juan Star*, the Governor was asked: "If Congress in a number of years, grants the presidential vote to all American citizens everywhere, would you resist it?"

The Governor answered, "No, no. My position is that, assuming that we develop Commonwealth, if such an initiative were to come to Puerto Rico, it would represent an additional development of Commonwealth."[10]

This contrasts markedly with his refusal nine years later to include Puerto Rico in H.R. 23 of January 5, 1985, which would have extended the presidential vote to all U.S. flag territories.

Defeated in 1976 by a pro-statehood candidate for governor, and bitterly disappointed by the failure of Congress to approve his Pact of Permanent Union with the United States, which represented the major effort of his administration over a four-year period, Hernández Colón did not abandon the struggle to gain more autonomy for Puerto Rico within the framework of free association.

In 1978, he testified before the United Nations Decolonization Committee and worked with the Cuban delegation to the United Nations on the text of a resolution condemning U.S. policy toward Puerto Rico, in exchange for acknowledgment by the committee of free association (but not the type of free association which Commonwealth represents, if one reads the text carefully) as a legitimate option for self-determination of colonial peoples.[11]

Hernández Colón's major effort in the late 1970's was a new policy document which he called his New Thesis. It was made

43

public on Constitution Day, July 25, 1979. It was basically a campaign guide for the 1980 elections, but it did identify basic powers which he said Puerto Rico must exercise in order to control its destiny:

1. Discretion on the administration of federal aid to the island, which it would receive in the form of a block grant;
2. Control of immigration;
3. Control of natural resources;
4. Protection of agriculture from outside competition; and
5. Control of radio and television.[12]

Failure to regain the governorship in 1980 by a narrow margin, and the entry of a pro-statehood president into The White House, was a double blow to Hernández Colón. His only consolation was that the Popular Democratic Party gained control of both houses of the state legislature. From this power base, the party was in a position to block any constitutionally meaningful moves toward statehood by the re-elected pro-statehood governor.

In the light of his later enthusiasm for President Reagan's Caribbean Basin Initiative, it is interesting to note his early opposition to this regional development program, as expressed in an article distributed by New York Times Special Features in mid-1982.[13]

Hernández Colón wrote as follows: "As the C.B.I. stimulates industrial development in Caribbean countries, they will export manufactured products to the United States, encroaching on those markets that now provide Puerto Rico with income and employment...The United States is not offering its own market to its Caribbean neighbors, but that of Puerto Rico...

"It is paradoxical that the United States should put forth a plan to stabilize the Caribbean Basin that will actually destabilize Puerto Rico...

"If C.B.I.'s effects are added to current problems, Puerto Rico will suffer social upheaval that will create opportunities for those who advocate violent change."

In a speech to the Rotary Club of San Juan two years later he was quoted as saying, "I agree with and support many of President Reagan's policies, particularly his effort to secure peace and stability in the Caribbean Basin and Central America."[14]

In fairness to Hernández Colón, it must be stated that the

President had met many of Puerto Rican's concerns in that two-year interval. On the other hand, it should be noted that he was in full campaign before a pro-United States audience. Then, too, he might have gotten wind of the fact that the U.S. Treasury was planning to eliminate Section 936 of the U.S. Internal Revenue Code and had already been thinking of the possibility of putting 936 funds in Puerto Rican banks to work in support of the ailing C.B.I. as a means of saving Section 936.

On another matter, Hernández Colón wrote in *The New York Times* of January 26, 1981: "The Commonwealth Party which I preside... is ready for a second plebiscite at any time." This position was reversed the following year when he claimed that a status plebiscite would seriously hamper economic recovery in Puerto Rico. He was quoted as saying, "The long and tempestuous process of trying to win statehood could bring investment to a virtual standstill and result in political violence from the more radical sectors."[15] The situation would leave the country unprotected and prostrate, he stated.

It was in 1983 that Hernández Colón adopted the position, reaffirmed in the Popular Democratic Party platform of 1984, and many times since, that if he were elected in 1984, he would not seek to alter the status of Puerto Rico for four years.

During the 1984 campaign, Hernández Colón expressed complete support of U.S. foreign policy, to the extent of drawing fire from the autonomous wing of his party.[16]

"Our commitment to Puerto Rico and the United States is one and the same, inseparable," he stated. "I will cooperate fully with the federal government to maintain democracy and freedom in the Caribbean."[17]

He came out specifically in support of the United States rescue mission in Grenada and U.S. policy in Central America, including aid to the *contra* rebels in Nicaragua.

The tone of Hernández Colón's second term as governor was set in his inaugural address on January 2, 1985. He reiterated a commitment made in the Popular Democratic Party platform and in his own campaign for governor that "we will not promote any plebiscite, referendum or political process whatsoever aimed at changing or altering our relationship as a Commonwealth of the United States."[18]

Hernández Colón presaged an active role in the Caribbean:

"Puerto Rico has an important role to play in advancing the cause of democracy among the Caribbean countries. We are going to assume a leadership role to attain those valuable objectives pursued by President Reagan's Caribbean Basin Initiative...

"Let us become an active and creative protagonist in the promotion of economic development, of economic stability, and of democracy in this region. Let us lend a helping hand to our Caribbean neighbors and at the same time, let us strengthen our own economy and development."

Then the bombshell: "Using funds deposited in the Government Development Bank by the 936 (federal tax-exempt) corporations, we will create an attractive financing mechanism to stimulate manufacturing processes initiated in other Caribbean countries and which would be finished, in their more technical and sophisticated phases, in Puerto Rico."

This is the idea of complementary production, popularly known as "twin plants." The unfinished product enters Puerto Rico, and accordingly, the U.S. tariff area, at little or no duty. Puerto Rico benefits, at least in theory, by the creation of high technology jobs on the island.

In the succeeding months, 42 twin plants were placed in operation, most of them in Haiti, the Dominican Republic, Antigua and Barbados.

On a related subject, Hernández Colón has endorsed in principle the recurrent idea of forming a Caribbean Parliament. But whether or not Puerto Rico joins, he said, depends on what kind of a parliament is formed. If it has decision-making powers, Puerto Rico, as a commonwealth of the United States, could not be a member. But if it is just a forum for discussion, Puerto Rico could join, he asserted.[19]

The Governor was steadfast in his determination not to ask for changes in Puerto Rico's status during the quadrennium. He said the Popular Democratic Party would wait until 1988 before deciding on its status plank for that year's election.[20]

Hernández Colón did not request greater autonomy for Puerto Rico during his second term. Instead, he decided to exercise some of the powers that he had asked for in the past but had been denied, especially in the foreign policy field. He insisted that "Puerto Rico maintain its own profile, its own personality and act with a certain independence from the United States, even in international affairs."[21]

His failure to coordinate fully with the U.S. Department of State with respect to a commercial and cultural agreement with Costa Rica got him in some trouble. The United States insisted on some modifications before it went into effect.

Speaking in Madrid, Governor Hernández Colón said his government would continue a policy of political autonomy but not independence from the United States.[22] It should be noted that in the lexicon of Hispano-american politics, a distinction is made between the words, "autonomy" and "independence." Autonomy signifies a high degree of self-government short of independence.

At Constitution Day ceremonies in 1985, Hernández Colón stated:

"The Free Associated State is a political organization that understands that its destiny is associated with the United States of America and whose mission is close and reciprocal cooperation with all of the Americas.[23]

The Commonwealth's Fourth of July celebration in 1986 was perhaps the first-ever commemoration of our nation's birthday where the U.S. flag was not prominently displayed on the reviewing stand. Neither was the Puerto Rican flag displayed, for that would have required the display of the U.S. flag. No White House representative was invited to the ceremony, as had been the practice in the past.[24]

On the other hand, President Jorge Blanco of the Dominican Republic was invited to speak at the Constitution Day ceremonies three weeks later.

In November 1985, for the first time in history only the Puerto Rican anthem was sung and the Puerto Rican flag displayed at an official function of the Government of Puerto Rico as Governor Hernández Colón addressed a gathering of 30,000 students.[25]

On the plus side, it should be noted that Governor Hernández Colón has continued to be a staunch supporter of U.S. policy in the Caribbean Basin. His willingness to invest 936 funds in the region in support of the President's C.B.I. program, while done principally to salvage the 936 tax exemption for Puerto Rico, has the potential of equaling the amount of funds invested by the U.S. Government in that same program. He has supported the U.S. position in the World Court in the legal action brought against the United States by Nicaragua. When asked if he would agree to sending Puerto Ricans to war against the Sandinista regime, he said he would be opposed, but would act only in cooperation with groups similarly opposed in the United States. With respect to the question of nuclear weapons at Roosevelt Roads, the Governor has accepted U.S. assurance that no nuclear weapons are stored there. "There are certain things," he said, "which require us to have confidence in the United States."[26]

Position of Severo Colberg

Severo Colberg is a former Speaker of the House of Representatives of Puerto Rico who in 1984 resigned this post, as well as key positions within the Popular Democratic Party, so as not to be bound by the party's policy of not discussing status during the 1984-1988 quadrennium.

As a result, Colberg has spoken and written widely and with great candor and conviction on status matters, and he has become the apostle of the autonomous wing of his party. His views are well known and they generally differ greatly from those of the Governor and the official party position.

Colberg's position on the political status of Puerto Rico can be summed up as follows: He considers the present relationship between Puerto Rico and the United States to be colonial and wishes to reduce U.S. influence in Puerto Rico. His demands include the removal of the U.S. District Court from Puerto Rico; control over territorial waters to a distance of 200 miles; control over minimum wage, immigration, civil aviation and banking; membership in UNESCO; a separate Olympic identity; a transfer of political power from the United States to Puerto Rico; and a treaty relationship with the United States as sovereign equals.

Colberg believes in maximum self-government for Puerto Rico but would want to retain common citizenship and common currency. He prefers a relationship to the United States along the lines of the Compact of Micronesia and the Marshall Islands, in his words, an associated republic. He favors developing mechanisms for economic independence and self-sufficiency, free of dependence on outside capital. He wants greater participation in international affairs, for example, the power to negotiate commercial, scientific and cultural treaties. He is in favor of United Nations resolutions that demand Puerto Rican self-determination as a matter of justice, rather than resolutions attacking the United States. He strongly condemns U.S. policy in Central America.[27]

In 1985, Colberg was personally invited by Castro to participate in a conference on the external debt of Latin America and the Caribbean. He was given a seat on the principal dias, just a few meters from Castro and his brother, Raúl. In a talk of about 30 minutes, Colberg, who speaks loudly against U.S. militarism in Puerto Rico, addressed Fidel Castro seven times by his military title, "Comandante."

The following excerpts from this speech capture the feelings of Colberg with respect to the United States and the political status of Puerto Rico:

"We have encountered here our own kind of blood, which is not northamerican. Our blood is iberoamerican, Caribbean...

"I have always considered full autonomy as our political route, but I have not discarded as an alternative, within this same process of self-determination, independence for Puerto Rico...

"Our sovereignty finds itself captive in the gluttonous and insatiable cage of northamerican imperialism."

On arrival at Muñoz Marín International Airport after a two-week stay in Cuba, Colberg told reporters: "I am an autonomist but I have always seen that after autonomy, there's an additional step that can be taken: independence."[28]

Colberg is in agreement with Senator Rubén Berríos, president of the Puerto Rican Independence Party, that the transformation of Puerto Rico into an associated republic can serve as a transitional step toward independence.

Colberg has termed the U.S. Federal Court in Puerto Rico an agent for the annexation and americanization of Puerto Rico. The Federal Court, he says, should not only keep out of Puerto Rican affairs; it should be physically removed from the island. Hernández Colón has called upon the federal judiciary to exercise a greater degree of deference to Puerto Rican law, but has stopped short of requesting the removal of the court from the island.

Colberg has vehemently opposed the construction of a Voice of America transmitter at Cabo Rojo, a small town in his district in southwest Puerto Rico. He has called the planned transmitter a CIA-backed effort to transmit military propaganda to Latin America.[29] Colberg has said that the federal government's "unilateral decision to expropriate privately-owned land for this purpose" violates the supposed compact between Puerto Rico and the United States.

On this point, Governor Hernández Colón differs with Colberg. The Governor recognizes that the federal government has the authority to acquire land in Puerto Rico for this purpose.

Colberg has also opposed establishment of a marine sanctuary by the federal government at La Parguera, located in the same general area. He feels that the U.S. military wants to use this area as a military training ground.

Hernández Colón has steered clear of the United Nations since his 1978 error in cooperating with the Cuban delegation, which was one factor in his failure to regain the governorship in 1980. But Colberg has testified before the UN Decolonization Committee a number of times, always as an individual. In 1981, he asked the committee to recommend that the "Puerto Rican case" be reconsidered by the United Nations General Assembly, and in 1985 he persuaded Venezuela to co-sponsor, with Cuba, a resolution calling for Puerto Rican independence.[30]

In both cases, Hernández Colón made it clear that Severo Colberg was acting in a personal capacity and that his views did not represent the position of the Popular Democratic Party nor the Government of Puerto Rico.[31] But a year later, in Caracas, Hernández Colón was reported to have congratulated Venezuelan leaders for their efforts at the United Nations on behalf of Puerto Rico. And in Lima, Perú, at the inauguration of the new president, Alan García, Hernández Colón chose not to set the record straight when García, in his inaugural address, called for Puerto Rican independence.

In 1985, Colberg defied Hernández Colón once more when he introduced a joint resolution in the Puerto Rican House of Representatives to ask the United States to petition UNESCO for Puerto Rican associate membership. In view of U.S. withdrawal from

UNESCO, Hernández Colón said he would veto the resolution if it were passed.[32]

Although the Popular Democratic Party has blown hot and cold with respect to participation in U.S. presidential primaries, Colberg has been consistent in opposing such participation.[33] He is also against extending the vote for U.S. president and vice president to U.S. citizens in Puerto Rico.[34]

In 1982, Severo Colberg and Rubén Berríos agreed on a ten-point economic program for Puerto Rico. Five of these points involved relations with the United States:

1. Full authority for Puerto Rico in determining commercial tariffs.
2. Full authority to sign treaties with foreign countries.
3. Termination of the applicability of U.S. maritime law to Puerto Rico.
4. Puerto Rico to establish the priorities for the use of federal funds on the island.
5. Control of indiscriminate immigration.[35]

Upon his return from Havana in 1985, Colberg called for the cancellation of Puerto Rico's $8 billion debt to the United States and for 20 years of U.S. economic aid until the Puerto Rican economy is stabilized.[36]

Severo Colberg has introduced measures in the past to make Spanish the official language of Puerto Rico and supports a similar bill introduced in 1986 by Senate Vice President Sergio Peña Clos. The measure is opposed by Hernández Colón.[37]

With respect to U.S. policy in the Caribbean, Colberg has said, "I condemn the use of Puerto Rico to invade Grenada. I think that military action was abusive." He said he was also against "the undue intervention [of the United States] in Nicaragua's affairs and in the Caribbean and the rest of Central America."

Colberg said that President Reagan "has resorted to big stick politics. The United States thinks it owns this hemisphere. It is a terrible error for Reagan to intervene unilaterally in other countries because of their politics. All Puerto Ricans should condemn this..."[38]

In 1985 Colberg introduced a resolution, subsequently passed by the House of Representatives, calling for an investigation of

U.S. military contingency plans for Puerto Rico.[39] He has accused Hernández Colón of going along with U.S. military plans in the Caribbean in exchange for keeping intact Section 936 of the U.S. Internal Revenue Code.[40]

He has criticized the commander of the National Guard of Puerto Rico for saying he would send contingents of the Guard to Central America if ordered to do so.[41] He believes Puerto Rico should have the right to decide if it will or will not participate in military conflicts in which the United States is involved, and the conditions under which the United States can retain bases on Puerto Rican territory.[42]

Colberg's views of Hernández Colón and his agenda after 1988, as expressed in a radio interview June 21, 1986 and reported in San Juan newspapers the next day, are of special interest.

Governor Hernández Colón, he said, is as much an autonomist as he is. Said Colberg, "He wants to pass into history as the person who culminated Commonwealth."

The status of Puerto Rico is already changing, said Colberg, with the governor's initiatives abroad, and these will move into high gear after the governor's re-election in 1988.

Richard Copaken, who was the main force in driving the Navy out of Culebra, will play an important role in the status change, says Colberg, who noted that Copaken recently negotiated a very liberal free association agreement for Micronesia.

When the associated republic is established, the Popular Democratic Party will make sure that the U.S. Navy and the U.S. District Court are completely removed from Puerto Rico, he said. He called the court an agent of North American imperialism and a "lance stuck into the side of the free associated state, which must be removed."

The free associated republic will also establish Puerto Rico's right not to participate in U.S. wars, "declared or undeclared." Compulsory service will never again exist in Puerto Rico.

Major changes will be made during Hernández Colón's third term, from 1988 to 1992, Colberg said. Hernández Colón will revive his New Thesis and demand control over immigration and the right to make treaties, and eliminate the applicability of U.S. maritime law to Puerto Rico.[43]

Position of other key leaders

The strongest and perhaps the most loyal follower of Hernández Colón is Miguel Hernández Agosto, president of the Senate and Vice President of the Popular Democratic Party.

So it came as a surprise to most political observers to read on July 14, 1986 the text of an interview granted by Hernández Agosto to *El Mundo*, a pro-government daily. First, the interview broke the party's vow to silence on the status issue. Secondly, Hernández Agosto appeared to suggest an early lifting of the vow when he said that status should be one of the issues in the 1988 elections.

"I personally believe that it would be very difficult for our party to participate in the 1988 elections without giving any attention to the question of status," he opined.

"It is necessary to examine relations, especially of the economic variety, between the United States and Puerto Rico," he said. Surprisingly, he included a plebiscite in the forthcoming quadrennium as a possibility. Up to then, the Popular Democratic Party had been ignoring calls for a plebiscite being voiced by proponents of statehood. He mentioned a constitutional convention as another alternative, but warned that such an assembly could only deal with the existing Commonwealth constitution, thus excluding discussion of statehood or independence.

Hernández Agosto said he personally favored a new Federal Relations Act, but if all options are to be examined, he was inclined to favor a plebiscite that would include the three options.

He personally favors a new bilateral agreement between the government of the United States and the people of Puerto Rico and cites the following areas as bearing urgent revision:

1. *The tariff system*. "Puerto Rico should have mechanisms to deal with exceptions in the U.S. tariff system. If we import raw materials to process and to create employment, we should try to import that material at the lowest possible price."

2. *Maritime law*, which prevents Puerto Rico from using ships of foreign registry for its commerce. "There are two alternatives: Either exempt Puerto Rico from U.S. maritime law, or provide aid or subsidy, as is given the U.S. merchant marine on international routes."

3. *Regulations of communication media*. "Communications in

Puerto Rico should respond to our country's culture."

4. *Supervision of environmental quality*. "I don't see why in Puerto Rico federal agencies should have any input. It's something Puerto Rico should control, and the United States would be losing nothing."

5. *Immigration*. "It's the establishment of mechanisms to insure that Puerto Rico is not inundated with immigrants that aggravate our problem of unemployment."[44]

These five points, which would represent adjustments in the existing Commonwealth arrangement, are Popular Democratic Party demands of long standing. The few differences that can be detected between Hernández Agosto and Hernández Colón are mostly in terms of emphasis. Hernández Agosto is slightly more autonomous in his views. For example, he is completely against presidential primaries in Puerto Rico in contrast to the Governor's policy of selective participation. He is willing to fight breaches of the U.S.-Puerto Rican "compact" in federal court, while Hernández Colón takes a pragmatic rather than a legalistic approach to the defense of Puerto Rico's rights.

With respect to Puerto Rican participation in U.S. wars, Hernández Agosto said in 1984: "I am definitely against the use of any Puerto Ricans in any belligerent expedition by the United States in Latin America. The Government of the United States should understand that Puerto Rico is united to Latin America by blood ties."[45] In early 1985, emerging from a conference with Hernández Colón on the subject, Hernández Agosto had softened his position. He said he favored a "consultative process" before Puerto Ricans are sent to fight in U.S. wars.[46]

Other *Populares*, otherwise loyal to Hernández Colón on most other matters, have not agreed with his opposition to the presidential vote for the people of Puerto Rico. The party's majority leaders in both the House and Senate, Rep. Presby Santiago and Sen. Gilberto Rivera Ortiz, have spoken out in favor of the vote. Popular Democratic Party Senator Gladys Rosario de Galarza estimated that the majority of her party in the Senate favors the vote.[47]

Populares whose views are more likely to coincide with those of Severo Colberg rather than those of Hernández Colón, at least in substance if not in intensity of conviction, include Senators

Sergio Peña Clos, Francisco Aponte Pérez, Victoria "Melo" Muñoz and Antonio Faz Alzamora and House Speaker José "Rony" Jarabo.

Sergio Peña Clos, Vice President of the Senate, admits to possible traces of colonialism in U.S.-Puerto Rican relations. He, too, identifies areas in which improvements can be made without waiting until 1988: greater control of communications media; permission to use non-U.S. ships in commerce between Puerto Rico and the mainland; control of immigration of foreigners into Puerto Rico; and international treaty-making.[48]

On April 22, 1986, Peña Clos introduced a bill which would have repealed a 1902 law establishing both English and Spanish as official languages in Puerto Rico. The bill would have made Spanish the only official language and would have required its use in all local government agencies.[49] The project was opposed by both Hernández Colón and Hernández Agosto and died in committee without hearings being held.[50] Hernández Colón said that "no one can change the fact that the language of Puerto Rico is Spanish, but at this moment it is not convenient to abolish English as a second official language."[51] Peña Clos is also against a federal court in Puerto Rico,[52] and he is in favor of the transfer of the Caribbean National Forest at El Yunque from federal to local jurisdiction.[53] He has introduced a bill to change Labor Day in Puerto Rico to May 1.[54]

Francisco Aponte Pérez, chairman of the Senate Judiciary Committee, has recommended amendments to the Federal Relations Act in three areas:

1. Puerto Rico should have power to make treaties with other countries of the Caribbean. As an example, he mentioned the San José Agreement which allows Caribbean nations to purchase oil at lower prices from Venezuela and Mexico.
2. Puerto Rico should be allowed to join international organizations such as CARICOM (the Caribbean Community), the Central American Common Market, and the Andean Pact.
3. Puerto Rico should be able to raise tariffs to protect its agricultural products.[55]

Aponte Pérez favors close examination of the Compact of Free Association of Micronesia and the Marshall Islands to see if some of its provisions can be applied to Puerto Rico.[56]

Victoria "Melo" Muñoz, daughter of the famous founder of the Commonwealth free association formula, was sworn in as Senator on July 11, 1986. She has been a maverick within the party and was not the first choice of Hernández Colón to fill the vacancy left in the Senate with the shift of Justo Méndez to a cabinet post.

Following is a summary of Senator Muñoz' past positions with respect to U.S.- Puerto Rican relations:

1. She is opposed to the use of Puerto Rican soil for the purpose of training troops for combat in Central America;[57]

2. She equates transit of nuclear arms through Puerto Rican waters with having nuclear arms in Puerto Rico, in violation of the Treaty of Tlatelolco.[58]

3. She is opposed to the extension of the presidential vote to Puerto Rico.[59]

4. She does not object to the installation of VOA antennas at Cabo Rojo but feels that the Commonwealth Government is ceding too much land for this purpose.[60]

5. She believes, as does Peña Clos, that an effort should be made in this governmental quadrennium to acquire more powers for the Free Associated State and cites amendments to U.S. maritime laws as one example.[61]

6. She favors the continued operation of the U.S. Federal Court in Puerto Rico.[62]

7. She flatly rejects independence as a solution to Puerto Rico's status dilemma.[63]

8. She favors establishing Spanish as the island's official language.

9. She has called for a "mechanism" whereby Puerto Ricans can decide if they wish to participate in conflicts in which the United States is involved.[64]

10. She favors leaving the Caribbean National Forest under federal administration.[65]

The following, excerpted from an interview with The San Juan Star, is revealing of her attitude toward the United States:

Could she be characterized as anti-American, pro-American, a little of both, or neither?

"I admire and respect the people of the United States," the senator said. "I'm for some of the policies of some of the presidents and against some of the policies of some of the other presidents. I think the United States is a great country. I admire how it has dealt with Watergate and racism since 1960, how the U.S. deals with its problems through the courts.

"I'm proud of Puerto Rico's relationship with the United States and of my American citizenship..."

And suppose she had to choose tomorrow between independence and statehood?

"You can't give me two choices I feel are destructive," Muñoz said. "Independence would mean extreme economic hardships, while statehood would translate not only into economic hardships, but cultural suicide. In fact," she added, "I think it is unjust for the United States to be asked to accept trouble by incorporating a Spanish-speaking country going under the guise of a state."[66]

Senator Antonio Faz Alzamora was recently named Secretary General of the Popular Democratic Party. He, too, has pledged to take the necessary steps to acquire more power for Puerto Rico in this quadrennium. He believes that Puerto Rican autonomists should continue their trips to the United Nations to defend development of Commonwealth status.[67]

House Speaker José "Rony" Jarabo has demonstrated a good deal of independence from the governor. He has introduced three bills to establish a 200-mile limit for Puerto Rican territorial waters, amendments to laws dealing with fishing, mining and ports. He has opposed the establishment of a federal wild life sanctuary at La Parguera.[68] He has asked Congress to set up a Permanent Commission on Puerto Rican Affairs to monitor federal regulations that restrict the island's economic development.[69] He is constant with Hernández Colón and Hernández Agosto, however, in his opposition to the presidential vote for Puerto Rico and to the establishment of Spanish as the official language of the island.[70]

Position of PROELA

PROELA (Pro-Estado Libre Asociado) is a private political organization allied to the Popular Democratic Party, designed to promote maximum political autonomy for Puerto Rico. Senator Aponte Pérez founded the organization in 1976, and was its president for the first five years. Severo Colberg and several other autonomy-minded legislators are also members. Representatives of PROELA have repeatedly testified at hearings of the United Nations Decolonization Committee. In so doing, they have assumed a position contrary to that of the Popular Democratic Party, which insists that the question of Puerto Rico's status is an internal matter between the United States and Puerto Rico. It has continually protested U.S. failure to honor Puerto Rican requests for modifications in the present Commonwealth status.

In 1982, PROELA supported a Cuban resolution asking that the UN General Assembly consider the Puerto Rican question as a separate item on its agenda. In 1985, it endorsed the Cuban-Venezuelan resolution calling for Puerto Rican independence, feeling that it also recognized the legitimacy of free association as a means of self-determination.[71]

PROELA has taken a position against the presidential vote for Puerto Rico while calling for the removal of the U.S. District Court from Puerto Rico. Its president, Carlos Vizcarrondo, has said that Puerto Rico should ask for the political status of an associated republic.[72]

Position of the United States

The basic position of the United States with respect to the free association option, indeed, all status options, is based on the universally-accepted principle of self-determination of peoples, as proclaimed by Woodrow Wilson in his Fourteen Points and enshrined in the Covenant of the League of Nations and the Charter of the United Nations. Every U.S. President since Dwight D. Eisenhower, and the U.S. Congress, in a joint resolution dated August 3, 1979, has pledged to respect the freely and democratically expressed will of the people of Puerto Rico with respect to their future.

In practical terms, the options have been independence, statehood and free association. Since free association was chosen by the people of Puerto Rico in a referendum in 1952 and reaffirmed in a plebiscite in 1967, the United States has respected that choice.

The history of the Commonwealth relationship, however, demonstrates that the United States considers its pledge to respect the will of the people of Puerto Rico regarding their political future to apply to shifts from free association to statehood or independence but not necessarily to any and all changes sought within the free association framework. This conclusion is based on the refusal of Congress to pass the Fernos-Murray Bill of 1959 (H.R.5926) and the Pact for Permanent Union of the 1970's.[73]

This was also made clear in President Jimmy Carter's message to the people of Puerto Rico of July 25, 1978. He stated in this message that "whatever decision that the people of Puerto Rico wish to take — statehood, independence or Commonwealth, or modifications mutually agreed upon of this status — will be yours and achieved according to your own traditions in a democratic and peaceful manner."[74] But, the sentence contains a *non sequitur.* If something has to be "mutually agreed upon," it can not be completely "yours," meaning emanating exclusively from the people of Puerto Rico. Also, the fact that changes within the framework of Commonwealth would require U.S. agreement makes it likely that changes from Commonwealth to some other type of free association formula, for example, the so-called associated republic, would also require U.S. agreement.

Political leaders of Puerto Rico often express desire for change, even specific changes, but no formal request for change has been submitted to Congress since the demise of H.B. 11200. Therefore, the U.S. Congress has not felt obliged to take a specific position with respect to a change in status for Puerto Rico. In 1986, however, the Interior and Insular Affairs Committee of the U.S. House of Representatives held a series of hearings on U.S. territories, with a view of arriving at some policy recommendations. Its report is awaited with great interest.

Congressman Robert J. Lagomarsino of California has expressed himself strongly in favor of statehood for Puerto Rico.[75] Congressman Mark Siljinder of Michigan personally received over a quarter of a million petitions for statehood in the name of the U.S. Congress. The only high-level vocal support for Commonwealth in Congress has come from Senator Ted Kennedy, although, of course, all Members recognize the legitimacy of the present Commonwealth government.

In a Declaration to the People of Puerto Rico on January 12, 1982, President Ronald Reagan reaffirmed his personal belief in the benefit of statehood for both the people of Puerto Rico and the people of the United States. Under statehood, he said, the language and culture of the island would be respected.

Vice President George Bush campaigned in Puerto Rico in 1980 under the banner, "Statehood Now!" He has repeated his personal preference for statehood on a number of occasions, most notably at The White House in 1985 in a talk to about 100 members of Puerto Ricans in Civic Action, a Puerto Rican pro-statehood movement. But the President and Vice President believe that any initiative for change must come from Puerto Rico. They have said that they would strongly support a request for statehood if it is made, but they have made it clear that they, like all presidents since Eisenhower, would, above all, respect the will of the people of Puerto Rico, whatever it might be.

The U.S. Department of State felt compelled to express itself strongly on Puerto Rican participation in international affairs early in 1986 when Hernández Colón overextended himself by negotiating a tax-sparing agreement with the Government of Japan. In answer to a query from the U.S. Embassy in Tokyo, the Department said:

"1. Embassy's concern over the appropriateness of supporting Puerto Rico's efforts on behalf on a tax-sparing agreement with Japan and Ministry of Finance uncertainty over the competence of the Government of Puerto Rico to enter into such an agreement are well founded.

"2. In matters of foreign affairs, the Commonwealth of Puerto Rico is a territory of the United States and as such does not have the authority on its own to enter into international agreements. In addition, the U.S. opposes the principle of tax-sparing and does not enter into tax-sparing agreements with any country. Embassy cannot therefore provide any support to current Puerto Rican efforts to negotiate such an agreement with Japan.

"3. Embassy may advise correspondents and should advise MOF (Ministry of Finance) of these instructions. Department will independently apprise Michael A. Deaver and Associates and, separately, consult with Puerto Rican authorities on this matter. The Government of Puerto Rico had not previously consulted with the Department on this issue and Embassy's telegram was greatly appreciated. Embassy is requested to cable texts of both Governor Hernández' and Mr. Deaver's letters to the Department and Treasury." Signed, Shultz.[76]

In testimony before the U.S. House Interior and Insular Affairs Committee July 17, 1986, Michael G. Kozak, principal deputy legal advisor to the U.S. Department of State, stated:

"...states, territories and commonwealths, including Puerto Rico, have a responsibility to ensure that their actions are internationally consistent with the foreign policy set and pursued by the federal government."[77]

In contrast, Governor Hernández Colón's program to invest Section 936 funds in the Caribbean in support of the President's Caribbean Basin Initiative was well coordinated with The White House, the Department of State and other federal offices and as a result was very well received. President Reagan endorsed the Governor's proposal to establish twin plants in the Caribbean region and said the program has the support of Congress. On the other hand, the President warned that the future of Section 936 will depend on the success of the twin plant program. Reagan was clear on the amount of money he expects Puerto Rico to invest each year: $100 million.

The U.S. Treasury believes that tax exemption for U.S. firms investing in Puerto Rico should be based on a wage credit rather than on income credit. In a letter dated August 7, 1985, Margaret DeB Tutweiler, Assistant Secretary of the Department of the Treasury, wrote as follows:

"The present section 936 credit is based on income derived from Puerto Rico or the U.S. possessions. Therefore, its attractiveness is directly related to the amount of income the firm can generate in the possessions; there is no necessary link to the amount of economic activity carried on there. In contrast, the proposed wage credit is directly related to employment in the possessions. Increasing employment in the possessions has always been, and remains, the principal goal of section 936. Moreover, the proposed wage credit may be used to offset U.S. tax on any income (from the possessions, foreign countries, or the United States). Thus, it should be attractive to a much broader range of firms. The wage credit would be permanent, to provide certainty, and it would include an additional credit for wages paid in excess of the minimum wage, to cover more highly-skilled labor."[78]

This position still has strong support in Congress. If the Governor falters, there may be another review of Section 936 of the U.S. Internal Revenue Code in one or two years.

Free Association Prospects

In view of the demands of free association advocates and positions taken by the U.S. Government in relation to such demands, what are the prospects for change within the free association framework?

Free association is a legitimate expression of the right of self-determination of peoples. The United Nations has so indicated in two key resolutions on the subject: UNGA Resolution 742 (VIII) 1953 and UNGA Resolution 1541 (XV) 1960.

In Part Three of the Annex to Resolution 742, the United Nations General Assembly sets forth 15 factors to be used in judging if a territory has achieved free association on an equal footing with a metropolitan country. The Free Associated State of Puerto Rico meets ten of these criteria. It fails to meet the following five:

A.6.i. "if constitutional guarantees extend equally to the associated territory; ii) if there are powers with respect to certain matters constitutionally reserved to the territory or the central authority, and iii) if the territory participates on an equal basis in the approval of modifications in the constitutional regime of the State."

The facts are: 1) all U.S. constitutional guarantees do not extend equally to Puerto Rico; ii) there are powers reserved to the U.S. government; and iii) Puerto Rico can modify its own constitution (within limitations) but does not have equal input with respect to modifications of the U.S. constitution, or Law 600.

B.1. "Representation without discrimination in the central legislative organs, on the same basis as other inhabitants of other regions."

Puerto Rico has only a Resident Commissioner without vote in the U.S. Congress. The 50 U.S. states each have two Senators and from one to 45 Representatives, depending on population, all with the right to vote, in the U.S. Congress.

B.3. "Rights of citizenship, without discrimination, under equal conditions with the rest of the inhabitants."

Puerto Ricans are U.S. citizens but are denied certain rights and benefits enjoyed by citizens in the U.S. states, for example, the right to vote for President and Vice President of the nation and equal protection under the Fourteenth Amendment.

B.4. "The capacity of public officials of the territory to be admitted to all public posts of the central authority by nomination or election, on the same basis as those from other parts of the country."

In theory, at least, U.S. citizens residing in Puerto Rico can be nominated for President and Vice President of the United States but are not eligible to fill the post of Representative or Senator in the U.S. Congress.

C.4. "Local autonomy to the same extent and under the same conditions as that of other parts of the country."

As a territory, Puerto Rico does not enjoy the reserved powers of the Tenth Amendment to the U.S. Constitution. Its powers are limited by the Puerto Rican Federal Relations Act, a law of the U.S. Congress.

Principle VII of the Annex of UNGA Resolution 1541 (XV) reads as follows:

"Free association should be the result of a free and voluntary choice by the people of the territory concerned, expressed through informed and democratic processes. It should be one which respects the cultural characteristics of the territory and its peoples, and retains for the peoples of the territory which is associated with an independent state the *freedom to modify the status of the territory* [emphasis is that of the author] through the expression of their will by democratic means and through constitutional processes.

"The associated territory should have the *right to determine its internal constitution without outside interference* [emphasis is that of the author] in accordance with due processes and the freely expressed wishes of the people. This does not preclude consultations as appropriate or necessary under terms of the free association agreed upon."

In the application of the criteria of Principle VII to the Free

Associated State of Puerto Rico, two problems are presented:

First, the words, "freedom to modify the status of the territory" become troublesome because Public Law 600 and the Puerto Rican Federal Relations Act, which govern U.S.-Puerto Rican relations, are Acts of Congress and as such, can only be amended by that body. Also, the U.S. Constitution specifies that "The Congress shall have the power to dispose of and make all needful rules and regulations respecting the territory or other property belonging to the United States."

Second, it is not at all certain that the Free Associated State of Puerto Rico has the "right to determine its internal constitution without outside interference." According to Article VII, Section 3 of the Constitution of the Commonwealth of Puerto Rico, "Any amendment or revision of this constitution shall be consistent with the resolution enacted by the United States approving this constitution, with the applicable provisions of the Constitution of the United States, with the Puerto Rican Federal Relations Act and with Public Law 600, Eighty-first Congress, adopted in the nature of a compact." This provision would seem to give the Congress of the United States considerable power over the constitution of Puerto Rico.

It appears, then, that the Free Associated State of Puerto Rico does not meet some of the key criteria of these two UN resolutions. And it would take more than mere cosmetic changes to the Federal Relations Act to bring the Free Associated State of Puerto Rico in conformity with these criteria. When one remembers that the U.S. Congress refused to make even the minor changes of the Fernos-Murray Bill and the Pact of Permanent Union, serious doubt arises as to whether the United States would want to enter into a free association agreement which recognized the juridical equality of both parties.

Some autonomists call for the application to Puerto Rico of the recently negotiated Compact of Free Association between the United States and the Federated States of Micronesia and the Marshall Islands.

This Compact does grant to this island group some of the powers which Puerto Rico has demanded in the past, for example, general control over immigration, communications, foreign trade and foreign affairs. The United States commits itself to extensive economic aid to the islands, the continuance of most federal programs, assumption by the United States of all debts and liabilities of the new state, grants totalling more than $1.24 billion over a 15-year period; even application of Section 936 of the U.S. Internal Revenue Code.

But the United States retains full control of security and defense matters. U.S. law continues to apply to the islands in many spheres of activity, for example, environmental control. Economic development plans for the island group require the approval of the U.S. Government.

It must be remembered that Micronesia and the Marshall Islands are part of a Strategic Trust Territory assigned to the United Nations Trusteeship Council. Thus, the inhabitants have never been U.S. citizens and would not become U.S. citizens under the new Compact. The high degree of constitutional autonomy granted the islands is in part compensation for their lack of citizenship. It is highly questionable whether Puerto Rico would want to trade off U.S. citizenship for additional autonomy. Furthermore, if terms of the Micronesian pact were applied to Puerto Rico, the unrestricted flow of Puerto Ricans back and forth to the United States would cease, as well as unlimited access to the U.S. market. Puerto Rican products entering the United States could be taxed.

Autonomists say they would negotiate continuance of U.S. citizenship and the common market, but there is considerable doubt that the United States would make such a concession while giving up so much control over the island and its inhabitants.

Another consideration is the vast difference between Puerto Rico on the one hand and the Federated States of Micronesia and the Marshall Islands on the other. Puerto Rico has a homogeneous, well-educated population of 3.2 million persons living for the most part on a single, compact island. The Federated States of Micronesia and the Marshall Islands are populated by some 100,000 natives of various ethnic origins living on just a few of the more than 2,000 islands that make up the group, scattered over an ocean area as large as the continental United States but having a land area less than a quarter that of Puerto Rico.

The Pacific islanders are concerned with improving their lot. The United States is concerned with maintaining its strategic position in the Pacific. The trade-off is more self-government and economic benefits for the inhabitants in exchange for military bases and transit rights. There is no assurance that the United States would be as generous to Puerto Rico.

Finally, the United Nations has not yet acted on the strategic trust territory, which embraces not only Micronesia and the Marshall Islands, but also the Northern Marianas, which have already adopted free association on the Puerto Rican model, and Palau, which has not quite made up its mind. This matter comes under the jurisdiction of the United Nations Security Council, where the Soviet Union holds veto power.

The kind of free association which would, in practice, meet United Nations criteria is difficult to imagine. The only precedent in recent history seems to have been the short-lived United Arab Republic, a kind of confederation between Egypt and Syria in the 1950's. Egypt and Syria merged to form a new state which was recognized as such by the United Nations and the world at large. Egypt and Syria were dropped from the United Nations membership rolls and the United Arab Republic was added.

The new state only lasted a few years because, as so often happens in such a partnership, the stronger member eventually begins to dominate the weaker, causing the latter to withdraw. The fact that juridical equality exists is eclipsed by the fact that one member is economically and politically stronger than the other and thus is able to dominate the arrangement.[79] An associated republic between a super-power and a small island such as Puerto Rico is not realistic.

In conclusion, agreement on a free association arrangement that would at the same time be acceptable to the United States, Puerto Rico and the United Nations, though theoretically possible, appears highly unlikely. As a practical matter, there seem to be only two ways by which Commonwealth can be culminated, either through statehood or through independence, which are clear-cut and viable options.

NOTES

Chapter II

1. The three best sources of information on Popular Party demands with respect to Commonwealth status are the Pronouncement of Aguas Buenas of November 19, 1970; the Pact for Permanent Union (HB 11200, 84th Congress, 2d Session, as amended, 1976); and Puerto Rican House of Representatives Concurrent Resolution 22 of March 21, 1982. All three are discussed in this chapter.

2. p. 3, *The San Juan Star*, July 9, 1984. Article, "PDP platform calls for no status change."

3. p. 3, *The San Juan Star*, April 23, 1983.

4. p. 34, *The San Juan Star*, May 7, 1985.

5. See two-part series on "The Hidden Agenda," *The San Juan Star*, p.26, January 27, and p. 16, January 28, 1986.

6. See articles, "Independentistas rock PDP," and "Party realignment," p. 25 and p. 26, respectively, of *The San Juan Star*, August 3, 1985 and April 28, 1986.

7. For the complete text of the Pronouncement of Aguas Buenas, see *Hearings before the U.S. Advisory Group on the Presidential Vote for Puerto Rico*, U.S. Government Printing Office, Washington, D.C. 1971, pp. 692-696 in Spanish and pp. 696-700 in English.

8. pp. 8-A and 9-A, *El Mundo*, April 28, 1974 and pp. 32, 47 and 50, *The San Juan Star*, April 28, 1974.

9. Lecture, "Puerto Rico's Presence and Participation in the World Community," Yale University, April 2-4, 1974.

10. p. 4, Outlook Section, The *San Juan Star*, August 8, 1976.

11. Official Documents of the General Assembly, 33d Period of Sessions, Supplement No. 23, (A/33/23) Chapter I, par. 66, September 12, 1978.

12. For complete text of the New Thesis, see page 14-A and 16-A of *El Mundo*, July 26, 1979.

13. See Outlook Section, *The San Juan Star*, June 27, 1982.

14. p. 12, *The San Juan Star*, September 19, 1984.

15. p. 1, *The San Juan Star* and p. 1, *El Mundo*, May 5, 1983.

16. p. 44, *The San Juan Star*, November 24, 1983, article, "The New Hernández Colón."

17. Speech before the Rotary Club of San Juan, as reported in *The San Juan Star*, September 19, 1984.

18. For full text in English, see p. 5 and 7, *The San Juan Star*, January 11, 1985.

19. p. 3, *The San Juan Star*, May 20, 1985.

20. p. 1, *The San Juan Star*, June 29, 1986.

21. pp. 52 and 57, *El Nuevo Día*, March 1, 1986, article "Hernández Colón looks at the Caribbean"

22. p. 2, *The San Juan Star*, March 8, 1986.

23. p. 3, *El Mundo*, July 26, 1985.

24. See photo and article, p. 3, *El Nuevo Día*, July 5, 1986.

25. p. 55, *El Nuevo Día*, November 22, 1985.

26. p. 8, *El Nuevo Día*, February 16, 1985.

27. The best sources of information on Colberg's views on the political status of Puerto Rico are *El Nuevo Día*, pp. 2-3, December 10, 1984, and p. 49, August 9, 1985. The latter gives the text of the speech he gave in Havana on August 2, 1985.

28. p. 15, *El Nuevo Día*, August 7, 1985.

29. p. 36, *The San Juan Star*, July 18, 1985.

30. p. 6, *The San Juan Star*, August 15, 1981, and p. 18A, *El Mundo*, September 4, 1984.

31. p.8, *The San Juan Star*, September 3, 1984 and p. 10-A, *El Mundo*, September 4, 1984.

32. p. 11, *El Mundo* and p. 3, *El Nuevo Día* January 18, 1985.

33. p. 19-A, *El Mundo*, September 16, 1982.

34. p. 45, *El Nuevo Día*, March 31, 1986.

35. p. 1, *El Mundo*, March 19, 1982.

36. p. 8, *El Mundo*, August 7, 1985 and p. 1, *The San Juan Star*, August 3, 1985.

37. p. 34, *El Mundo*, June 12, 1986, and p. 29, *The San Juan Star*, June 12, 1985.

38. p. 14, *The San Juan Star*, September 20, 1984.

39. p. 5, *El Nuevo Día*, February 15, 1985.

40. p. 27, *El Nuevo Día*, May 5, 1985.

41. p. 8, *El Nuevo Día*, February 12, 1985.

42. p. 8, *El Nuevo Día*, August 7, 1985.

43. p. 2, *The San Juan Star*. June 22, 1986; p. 9, 14, *El Mundo*, June 22, 1986; and p. 9, *El Nuevo Día*, June 23, 1986; and p. 32, *The San Juan Star*, July 1, 1986.

44. pp 2, 3, *El Mundo*, July 14, 1986.

45. p. 3-A, *El Mundo*, December 3, 1984 and p. 3, *The San Juan Star*, March 20, 1985.

46. p. 10, *El Mundo*, February 16, 1986; p. 19, *El Nuevo Día*, and p. 8, *The San Juan Star*, February 3, 1986.

47. p. 9, *El Nuevo Día*, January 19, 1986.

48. p. 4, *El Nuevo Día*, July 29, 1985 and p. 11, *El Mundo*, April 21, 1986.

49. p. 3, *The San Juan Star*, April 23, 1986.

50. p. 15, *El Mundo*, June 1, 1986.

51. p. 16, *El Nuevo Día*, May 26, 1986.

52. p. 9, *El Nuevo Día*, June 9, 1986, and p. 9 *El Mundo*, June 9, 1986.

53. p. 25, *El Mundo*, February 27, 1987.

54. p. 11, *El Mundo*, March 15, 1987.

55. p. 30, *The San Juan Star*, May 1, 1985.

56. p. 47, *El Nuevo Día*, August 24, 1985.

57. p. 5-A, *El Mundo*, November 13, 1984.

58. p. 9, *El Nuevo Día*, February 19, 1985.

59. p. 16, *El Nuevo Día*, February 20, 1986 and p. 14, *The San Juan Star*, February 23, 1986.

60. p. 14, *The San Juan Star*, February 23, 1986.

61. p. 5, *El Mundo*, June 15, 1986.

62. p. 23, *El Mundo*, June 21, 1986.

63. *Ibid*.

64. p. 44, *The San Juan Star*, November 24, 1983.

65. p. 2, *The San Juan Star*, November 19, 1986 and p. 14, *El Mundo*, December 8, 1986.

66. p. 2, *The San Juan Star*, October 19, 1986.

67. p. 10, *El Mundo*, November 11, 1985.

68. p. 17, *El Mundo*, December 31, 1986.

69. p. 3, *El Nuevo Día*, February 1, 1985 and p. 2, *El Mundo*, February 1, 1985.

70. p. 10, *The San Juan Star*, May 23, 1986.

71. p. 13, *El Nuevo Día*, February 10, 1986 and p. 13, *The San Juan Star*, June 20, 1986.

72. p. 26, *El Mundo*, August 18, 1985.

73. HB 11200, 84th Congress, 2d Session, 1976.

74. p. 125, *Relaciones entre los Estados Unidos y Puerto Rico: Documentos Básicos*. Editorial Instituto Interamericano, Hato Rey, Puerto Rico, 1984. Revised, 1987.

75. Statement at Municipality of San Juan's Independence Day observance, July 4, 1986. On June 30, 1987, Congressman Lagomarsino introduced a pro-statehood bill in the U.S. House of Representatives.

76. U.S. Department of State Unclassified Outgoing Telegram P141813Z Ja 86.

77. Complete text of Kozak's testimony appears on pages 18 and 19 of *The San Juan Star*, July 20, 1986.

78. Excerpt from letter to the author.

79. For an unofficial translation of the Charter for the Creation of the United Arab States see Press Release of the Embassy of the United Arab Republic, Washington, D.C., March 10, 1953. For an evaluation of the experiment, see Kerr, Malcolm, *The Arab Cold War*, Oxford University Press, 1971, and the article, "The U.A.R., What Went Wrong?" Fauji M. Najjar, Vol. III, No. 2, *The Free World*, Free World Forum, Washington, D.C., 1961.

Chapter III

THE STATEHOOD OPTION AND
ITS PROSPECTS

The conversion of Puerto Rico into the 51st state of the United States of America is the principal aim of the New Progressive Party (NPP) of Puerto Rico, under the able leadership of San Juan Mayor Baltasar Corrada del Río.

The NPP considers Puerto Rico's current political status to be colonial, subject to the whim of the U.S. Congress under the territorial clause of the U.S. Constitution. The establishment of the Commonwealth in 1952 did not change that relationship, the party contends, because the basic provisions of the Organic Act of 1917 governing U.S.-Puerto Rican relations were retained under the Federal Relations Act.

The authority of the United States over Puerto Rico flows not from the consent of the governed, the NPP says, but from the Treaty of Paris, which transferred Puerto Rico from Spain to the United States as war booty, and from the territorial clause of the U.S. Constitution, which gives Congress full power over Puerto Rico.

A compact between the United States and Puerto Rico, in the sense of an immutable agreement between two parties, does not exist, according to advocates of statehood, because time and again the U.S. Congress has taken action adverse to the interests of Puerto Rico without consulting the people of Puerto Rico. Congress has also taken unilateral action discriminatory toward Puerto Rico, such as lowering nutritional assistance several hundred million dollars a year less than it would receive if accorded equal treatment. This would be impossible under statehood, the NPP points out, because the equal protection clause of the Fourteenth Amendment would be applicable.

The NPP views statehood as the natural culmination of Commonwealth and territorial status, and a natural right of U.S. citizens residing in Puerto Rico. The party regards a change to statehood as basic to the solution of the social and economic problems of the island.

Because the rights of U.S. citizens in Puerto Rico are less than those enjoyed by U.S. citizens on the mainland, advocates of statehood speak about a second-class citizenship for inhabitants of the island and regard statehood mainly as a question of civil rights and equality of citizenship. The different treatment accorded Puerto Rico under the territorial clause of the U.S. Constitution is a violation of basic rights of citizenship which can only be remedied by converting Puerto Rico into a state of the union, say statehood advocates. They feel that only statehood can bring about the fulfillment of all the rights of U.S. citizenship for the people of Puerto Rico.

The 1984 NPP platform emphasizes that no ethnic, racial or religious community has ever achieved economic and social equality within the nation-state without first having achieved political equality. The party believes that when Puerto Rico solicits admission into the federal union, Congress and the President will be morally and politically obligated to grant it.

The present situation, the party states, is undignified and intolerable. They say it amounts to geographical discrimination: a Puerto Rican in the United States enjoys the full rights of citizenship, but when he or she or any other U.S. citizen for that matter moves to the island of Puerto Rico, rights are lost, for example, the right to vote for President and Vice President of the nation, the right to equal representation in the U.S. Congress, and the right to equal treatment under federal laws and programs.

At present, the statehooders say Puerto Rico is in a squeeze. Because of U.S. budget cutting, the island is losing some of the privileges formerly received under Commonwealth status (some benefits from Section 936 of the U.S. Internal Revenue Code, and part of the tax on Puerto Rican rum sold in the United States, for example) while being harmed much more than would be the case if it were a state (for example, in the program of nutritional assistance).

The NPP agrees with the PDP that Puerto Rico should have the right to object to laws that affect the island adversely, but through the medium of two voting U.S. Senators and seven voting U.S. Representatives, to which it would be entitled as a state, rather than registering a governmental objection which Congress can refuse to honor.

The NPP estimates that in 1983 Puerto Rico lost at least $1.2 billion in benefits and $1.5 billion in sales to the federal government by not being a state of the union.[1] As a state the NPP states that Puerto Rico would be eligible for $60 million a year more in educational funds; $280 million a year more in health services; $422 million a year more in aid to the blind, handicapped and elderly; and additional federal funds for highways, housing, agriculture and environmental protection, plus Supplementary Security Insurance and Aid to Families with Dependent Children, which it is not now receiving under Commonwealth status.

In addition, the NPP points out that under statehood every worker would be guaranteed at least the U.S. minimum wage.

The NPP accepts the presence of the U.S. District Court in Puerto Rico as an absolute necessity under the Federal system of government. The conflicts between civil and common law, the party says, are more imaginary than real. The same judgments would result under both systems, no matter which system of law is applied, the party contends.

Statehood advocates are strongly in favor of participating in U.S. presidential primaries and U.S. elections and politics. They believe that Puerto Ricans should have the right to participate in the choice of the Chief Executive of the nation, who wields such strong powers of decision over all U.S. citizens and would be their commander-in-chief in time of war. They believe that Puerto Rican delegates to U.S. national party conventions can be used as bargaining chips for what Puerto Rico wants. They cite as an example the extension of Puerto Rican control over its territorial waters from three to 12 nautical miles in 1980. Senator Howard Baker, then Senate majority leader, introduced and guided this legislation through the Senate as an effort to win Puerto Rican votes in that year's presidential primary in Puerto Rico, and Jimmy Carter signed the bill into law in gratitude to pro-statehood Democrats who helped him win that same primary.[2]

The latest document embodying the NPP's basic ideas on statehood is the Government Program proposed by the party for the 1985-1989 quadrennium. As a campaign document, it exudes some of the party's fervor. A translation of the Declaration of Principles follows:

"Nearly five centuries after its discovery and 84 years under the American flag, Puerto Rico has not yet solved its colonial condition. We are a non-incorporated territory of the United States over which Congress, the President and the federal bureaucracy can exercise ample powers of sovereignty. A constitutional government of laws safeguards our personal liberties. However, in a collective sense, the will of others rules over our will.

"The concession of American citizenship in 1917 did not change the political and juridical subordination of the people of Puerto Rico to the Government of the United States. Neither did it change the actions that later emanated from the Organic Act which established, by Congressional decision, the actual territorial condition of the Free Associated State.

"As before, the authority of the United States over Puerto Rico does not emanate from the consent of our people, nor our participation in the decisions of the federal government, but rather from the Treaty of Paris of 1898 and the territorial clause of the U.S. Constitution, which gives full power for the Congress to decide the future of Puerto Rico as it deems necessary.

"Our relations with the United States rest on this precarious and unstable foundation. It is a colonial connection that does not correspond to our economic and social structure, with its deep ethnic, cultural and democratic roots, that have been an example of progress in the Americas.

"During the course of the present century, Puerto Rico has multiplied its wealth and increased its productive activity; has trained its human resources; has increased its cultural contacts with the rest of the nation and with the exterior and reaffirmed its identity; has fortified its pattern of democratic co-existence; and finally, has overcome its old image of 'The Poorhouse of the Caribbean.' In fact, we have grown in all cultural aspects, but with respect to our political and constitutional status, we still lack the rights of participation in the governmental processes which govern our lives. The lack of substantial growth in such a vital area now constitutes an impediment — a brake — on our continued growth and a threat to that which we have achieved.

"We should emphasize that, while our economic and social development has been great in relation to the past and with respect to that of the people of Latin America, Puerto Rico finds itself behind in its economic development in comparison with the United States.

"The question of status is not a question of more theories and abstract principles. On the contrary, it bears a close relationship to our daily lives. The solution of this problem depends on being able to reach those levels of progress and welfare, security and social stability for which our people yearn.

"This is proven by events relating to amendments to Section 936 of the U.S. Internal Revenue Code; excessive cuts in our assignment of funds for nutritional aid; and our meager participation, or lack of participation, in federal programs that assign benefits to the most needy citizens in the states of the union.

"This confirms the extent of federal powers over Puerto Rico and shows, in the case of amendments to Section 936, that a single congressional action in a brief moment is sufficient to affect the conditions for capital investment and economic development on our island and to offset our efforts in the area of industrial promotion. Other cases emphasize that electoral power and the representation which emanates from electoral power, constitute an indispensable condition for full enjoyment of our rights of citizenship. No ethnic, racial or religious community has ever reached economic and social equality within a nation without first having achieved political equality.

"From this perspective, we can appreciate the reality of Puerto Rico, and we can see that in order to reach our collective goals, it is essential to create the political bonds that unite us permanently to the United States. This means full citizenship, adding to it the full dignity of rights which give us participation in the process and in government bodies that determine on the federal level what Puerto Ricans must do. This participation, also critical to the preservation and strengthening of our culture, has reduced the sphere of jurisdiction and competence of the Free Associated State.

"Statehood is, then, the principal reason for existence of the New Progressive Party. The political condition we suffer does not satisfy us because we can not accept in perpetuity the legitimacy of federal power exercised without our participation and because we are not satisfied with incomplete citizenship, without its inherent political and economic rights. Neither can we accept the frailty of our political relationship with the nation, which affects the economic and social development of Puerto Rico.

"These conditions go to the root of the political problems of our people. The problem is obvious when we receive unequal and less favorable treatment in federal programs of economic development and social security as in programs of youth education and employment or to protect the blind, the handicapped, the elderly, the ill and poor families.

"Congress as well as the President has pledged to support the decision taken by the people of Puerto Rico to resolve their status dilemma. Congress has never considered statehood for Puerto Rico because our people have never petitioned for it. However, when a majority of the people of Puerto Rico asks for admission as part of the union, Congress and the President of the United States will be morally and politically obligated to grant us statehood.

"Our people's lack of political identification is the basic reason for many economic and social problems that we should correct as soon as possible through statehood. This has been the goal of our party since its origin, and this commitment constitutes the principal reason for being of the New Progressive Party.

"We want and need statehood

—Because we aspire to political equality within the American union.

—Because we need to exercise the right to vote for president and vice president and elect our senators and representatives to Congress, participate in the approval of laws which affect our lives and in the selection and confirmation of federal officials who make the decisions applicable to Puerto Rico.

—Because the rights of political participation inherent in citizenship and the power emanating from them constitute guarantees and defenses of our economic, social and cultural development, threatened today by the lack of power of the Free Associated State, which is consumed by its impotence, and

—Because in statehood Puerto Rico can conserve the characteristics which identify us as a separate people, that is, our language and our culture. We will also conserve our liberal institutions, politically and economically, and raise our standard of living, as well as our level of scientific and technological development, which forms part of our cultural identity.

—Because putting an end to indecision, we will put an end to antagonisms, to extreme politization, and to the division of the Puerto Rican family, and we can direct our collective efforts to the solution of our vital problems, and to the creation of a better civilization, with a sense of direction and unity of purpose.

"Statehood will give us the opportunity to conduct a peaceful social revolution. With this, we will achieve a better education, better opportunities, better conditions of health and housing and a more just distribution of wealth; in sum, a life with better guarantees of security and progress.

"To this end, the New Progressive Party will continue orienting and educating the public on the benefits, responsibilities and advantages of statehood.

"We urge the people of Puerto Rico to unite with our claim to equality and political dignity, and to express before the Congress of the United States their majority will to enter the union with all the rights, prerogatives and obligations which correspond to a state.

"The nation is its people, and the formula which best guarantees the welfare of the people of Puerto Rico, of all Puerto Ricans, is the equality and the sovereignty embodied in STATEHOOD. On this route, with the greatest sense of patriotic responsibility, Puerto Rico directs its steps toward the conquest of the rights that assure the welfare, the tranquility and the progress of the people of Puerto Rico, of each Puerto Rican.

"The New Progressive Party reaffirms its unbreakable commitment to STATEHOOD and proclaims that the struggle to achieve it permits neither hesitation nor delay."

The remainder of the program is devoted to specific areas of governmental activity. Each section concludes with a statement of the amount of additional funds Puerto Rico would receive to deal with problems in each area if Puerto Rico were a state of the union.[3]

On November 25, 1985, the New Progressive Party amended its rules to call for a status plebiscite if it wins the 1988 election. The plebiscite can take the form of a vote on statehood, yes or no; statehood versus independence; or a choice among the three status options, the party decided. If statehood wins, the party would petition the Congress for an Enabling Act with a transitional period of 20 years to make the necessary adjustment from Commonwealth.

Despite considering Puerto Rico's relationship with the United States to be colonial in nature, the New Progressive Party does not view the United Nations as the medium for bringing about a change in this situation. On the contrary, the party is confident that the United States will remedy the situation through statehood once the party is able to demonstrate that statehood indeed is the will of the people of Puerto Rico.

The three principal leaders of statehood thought on the island are San Juan Mayor Baltasar Corrada del Río, president of the New Progressive Party; and former governors Carlos Romero Barceló and Luis A. Ferré. Since statehood presents a single, clear-cut option (in contrast to free association, which presents a range of options), it has been easier for statehooders to unite on their status views. (This, however, has not prevented party leaders from quarreling among themselves on other matters, thus holding back progress toward the common ideal.) There follows a brief summary of the views of these three men, and of a few others, and of the work of an active citizens movement, Puerto Ricans in Civic Action.

Position of Baltasar Corrada del Río

Baltasar Corrada del Río served as U.S. Resident Commissioner to Congress from 1976 to 1984. In 1984, he was elected Mayor of San Juan, Puerto Rico's largest city and the capital of government, in a close election which saw the governorship and both houses of the legislature fall to the control of the Popular Democratic Party. Former Governor Carlos Romero Barceló took a political vacation, holding on to the title of president of the New Progressive Party, but designating Corrada as acting president, charged with reorganizing the party. On June 21, 1986, Corrada was elected president of the party in his own right.

Corrada demonstrated his contempt for Commonwealth as a status option from the moment he took office as mayor. He refused to take an oath to defend "the constitution and laws of the Free Associated State of Puerto Rico," swearing instead, to the applause of those in attendance, to defend "the constitution and laws of Puerto Rico."[4]

On July 17, 1985, in a speech at the tomb of Dr. José Celso Barbosa, recognized as the father of the Puerto Rican statehood movement, Corrada leveled an accusation against Governor Hernández Colón that left many people shocked, skeptical or both. Hernández Colón, he said, "holds the firm purpose, by means of a hidden and well planned agenda, to lead our people on a journey that will take them to an independent republic, through a new pact of free association between Puerto Rico and the United States to be signed sometime between 1989 and 1992.

"This strategy," he said, "represents the gravest danger to Puerto Rico's security, democracy and progress, and if successful, would eventually lead to the rupture of the bonds of union between Puerto Rico and the United States." He predicted that the Hernández Colón administration would try to use the Micronesian Compact of Free Association, then under Congressional consideration, as a kind of model for the establishment of an associated republic in Puerto Rico.

In subsequent months, there were indications that Corrada's analysis might be correct, as autonomists played a leading role in the Popular Democratic Party and the Governor intensified his activities in the international arena.

Corrada testified at the three hearings held by the U.S. House Interior and Insular Affairs Committee in 1986. In testimony at the April 10 hearing he said:

"A sensible federal policy toward the territories should return to the logical principles of the Northwest Ordinance, and away from the irrational and invidious incorporated-unincorporated distinction. Since the United States has no desire to become an imperial power and hold colonies in America, the U.S. policy toward its territories should be one of eventual incorporation into the union. The United States cannot excuse its moral and political responsibility toward Puerto Rico by simply stating its support for the principle of self-determination without making a commitment toward statehood as the only valid solution to the political status of Puerto Rico...

"Self-determination must have constitutional parameters. Independence, for example, is not a constitutional option for a community of U.S. citizens like Puerto Rico. To accept independence as an option would amount to stripping 3.3 million American citizens of their citizenship, something only comparable to allowing a state of the union to separate from the union and declare itself a sovereign republic. Furthermore, even though independence leaders are articulate and smart in presenting their viewpoints, only about five percent of the people would support independence. Our people simply do not want it.

"Commonwealth status, which has served as a transitional stage for statehood, can hardly be seen as a permanent status in itself unless the nation is willing to perpetuate political inferiority. Self-determination, hence, should be defined within a constitutional context as the right of American citizens residing in Puerto Rico to ask for statehood and the commitment of the United States to support it under conditions that are mutually acceptable."

Corrada asked the Interior Committee for

1. The extension of the presidential vote to all American citizens residing in the territories;
2. Parity of representation in the U.S. Congress;
3. An orderly transition or phase-in of the applicability of the U.S. Internal Revenue Code.
4. Equal treatment in federal programs.

Corrada went on to explain each of these proposals:

"The presidential vote is supported by the continuing efforts of the delegates of the flag territories that in each Congress move for its adoption. Time after time, substantial support is garnered for this measure, but its passage has not happened. This Congress must endorse the enactment of this essential right.

"The second proposal asks for the recognition of territorial delegates in proportion to the population represented. In the case of Puerto Rico, this would be seven territorial delegates admitted as members of Congress with the same rights and privileges currently enjoyed by the territorial delegates in this committee. On the Senate side, two territorial delegates to be admitted with similar prerogatives. All delegates are to be elected officials representing their particular district and territory.

"This full territorial delegation will insure Puerto Rico's input in the formulation of federal legislation and policies by increasing its political participation in the process. It will also instill in the Puerto Ricans the sense of direction and purpose which will culminate with full voting rights in the Congress under statehood.

"The third proposal is essential in order to resolve the current crisis in Puerto Rico's economic development. Since 1982, this Congress has made changes to Section 936 of the Internal Revenue Code and is currently contemplating additional modifications. The end result is that the industrial sector of Puerto Rico which spearheaded this island's economy has been threatened. This continuing uncertainty has driven a program which started as 'Operation Bootstrap' into almost total paralysis. Although that is not the intent or purpose of this Congress, it is the unfortunate result. This uncertainty is intrinsic of this 'holding pattern' we are in.

"In order to remove this uncertainty, the Internal Revenue Code has to be made to reflect the goal of statehood for Puerto Rico. A transition from a 'possession system' of taxation to eventual statehood must be mapped. This transition would recognize the grandfathering of Section 936, followed by the enactment of a new Internal Revenue Code designed to provide tax incentives as effective as that provided by the current 936 system. This is supported by the 'equal footing' doctrine of the statehood process.

"We must all recognize that Puerto Ricans currently carry a higher tax burden that the residents of the fifty states. Not all those taxes are covered to the U.S. Treasury. A period of transition has to be defined that will not increase the tax burden of the Puerto Ricans, and that will bring it in line with the state-federal tax relationship.

"Finally, the fourth proposal will extend equal treatment in federal programs to Puerto Ricans. As recently as 1980, the U.S. Supreme Court sustained differential treatment for the U.S. citizens in Puerto Rico pursuant to Article IV, Section 3 of the U.S. Constitution, the 'territorial clause,' which empowers Congress to 'make all needful rules and regulations respecting the territory.' It is my position that there is no rational basis to continue to provide program participation in a discriminatory fashion in Puerto Rico..."

Corrada asked Congress "to approve legislation offering statehood to Puerto Rico subject to the support of the majority of our people in a referendum." Such referendum on statehood would be called by the U.S. Congress with a commitment to respect the democratic and free expression of the majority of eligible voters participating in the referendum. If statehood wins, as it will, the terms of the statehood enabling act will be discussed and agreed upon with The White House and the Congress.

"Congress must finally recognize that the United States made a threshold decision when it granted American citizenship to Puerto Ricans in 1917, and that Commonwealth status is a traditional status, part of the so-called 'holding pattern' which should lead to our admission to the union as the fifty-first state. Congressional policy toward the territory of Puerto Rico must be based on that unavoidable and exciting reality. Our vision must be based on a great future of equality and dignity for the proud and hard-working people of Puerto Rico."

In hearings before the Committee on May 20, 1986, Corrada stated:

"The citizens of Puerto Rico and the Congress cannot begin effectively to solve the pressing socio-economic problems prevalent in the Commonwealth (both on a short-term and long-range basis) until the island's political status problem has been permanently solved. Until that happens, Congressional economic policy should be based on the objective of treating Puerto Rico as if it were a state."

Corrada, who is expected to be his party's candidate for Governor in 1988, has predicted that if he is elected, and if Vice President Bush is elected to the presidency, Congress "may be persuaded to back an act offering statehood to Puerto Rico and asking the people if they want it or not. "[5]

In his third appearance before the Interior Committee on July 17, 1986, Corrada renewed his accusation that Hernández Colón was leading Puerto Rico toward independence or an associated republic. He said that the governor was traveling about as Chief of State of an independent republic and signing treaties beyond the jurisdiction of the United States, trying to create "de facto" independence for Puerto Rico. He recited a list of pro-autonomy actions and statements over an 18-month period, concluding that Puerto Rico was being run by officials driven by "ideological schizophrenia. "[6]

Corrada has been a strong supporter of President Reagan's Caribbean Basin Initiative. He gave it strong endorsement in a speech to the Puerto Rican Chamber of Commerce on June 4, 1982, just three months after the plan was submitted to the Congress. However, as Resident Commissioner, he took steps to assure that the economy of Puerto Rico would be helped rather than hurt by the C.B.I.[7] In an article in *Foreign Policy* magazine in the summer of 1982, Corrada took the position that the C.B.I. was good for Puerto Rico; Hernández Colón took the position that it was bad.[8]

As Resident Commissioner, Corrada also fought for retention of Section 936 of the U.S. Internal Revenue Code. When the U.S. Treasury seemed determined to eliminate the section in late 1984, Corrada suggested incorporating the tax exemption in a long-term Statehood Enabling Act.[9] He suggested that the phasing out of Section 936 be accompanied by a phasing in of a new system of incentives compatible with statehood.[10]

Corrada also suggested that all of Puerto Rico could be made an enterprise zone in which companies would be given special tax exemption for setting up businesses.[11]

By mid-1986, when it seemed that Congress would leave Section 936 virtually untouched, Corrada had shifted his position. He pushed a resolution through the conference of U.S. mayors, meeting in San Juan, which unanimously supported the preservation of Section 936 without change.[12] Corrada, however, has opposed the use of 936 funds in Puerto Rican banks for Caribbean development, claiming that the Hernández Colón administration is endangering Puerto Rico's credit in risky projects in Caribbean countries.[13]

Corrada has opposed the constitutional amendment proposed by Popular Democratic Party Senator Peña Clos that would establish Spanish as the official language of Puerto Rico. As Resident Commissioner, he opposed a resolution by former U.S. Senator S.I. Hayakawa of California to make English the official language of the United States. His opposition to both bills was for the same reason. He felt that language should not be made an issue of patriotism. He recalled that Jimmy López, a Puerto Rican among the Americans held hostage in Iran, wrote in Spanish on a U.S. embassy wall, "Long live the Red, White and Blue."[14]

Corrada does not feel that Puerto Rico would lose its Olympic identity if it became a state. He said there is nothing in the Olympic charter that prohibits states or territories from separate representation in Olympic competition.

As for the storage of U.S. nuclear weapons in Puerto Rico, Corrada is opposed, but argues that Cuba and the Soviet Union pose the real threat to peace in the Caribbean. He has stated that the United States would have a right to take whatever action it deemed necessary, including by-passing the Tlatelolco Treaty, if a real nuclear threat surfaced from either country.

Corrada has supported the installation of a Voice of America relay transmitter in Cabo Rojo. "The Voice of America," he said, "has always been a very responsible medium, very serious, not of political propaganda."

Corrada opposes the training in Puerto Rico of *Contras* "and all other clandestine and private groups." However, he defends the training in Puerto Rico of regular army units. In such case, he says, "Puerto Rico should cooperate as part of its responsibility to defend democracy."

With respect to the Puerto Rican case at the United Nations, Corrada feels that statehood sentiment would increase on the island if the UN General Assembly should ever say that Puerto Rico is a U.S. colony. However, he shares the basic U.S position that the United Nations should not intervene because the issue should be resolved between the United States and Puerto Rico. The United States, he reminds, is committed to respect the right of self-determination for Puerto Rico.[17]

Corrada has said that he favors the use of the Tennessee Plan for joining the U.S. federal union. When a majority of Puerto Ricans want statehood, he would send seven Puerto Ricans to the U.S. House of Representatives and two to the U.S. Senate "to knock on doors and awaken the national conscience as to our rights."[18]

Position of Carlos Romero Barceló

Former Governor (1977-1985) and now a State Senator, Carlos Romero Barceló projects the classic image of the *caudillo* in Latin American politics; indeed, he is fondly known as the *caballo* for his custom of campaigning on horseback. His pro-statehood convictions are so strong that as Governor he once stated that he would ask the United States for statehood only once; if rebuffed, he would promptly ask for independence. Many considered this statement a weak attempt to blackmail the United States. But no one who knew Romero and his strong Latin sense of *dignidad* doubted his word. To Romero, the political status of Puerto Rico is essentially a civil rights question, a problem of geographical discrimination.

To those who admire the strong man in politics, Romero is a hero. Those who prize finesse find him abrasive. That he lost the governorship in 1984 was the consequence of a public test of strength with a contender for the nomination. He won the nomination but lost the governorship because the loser went off, formed his own party and drained off enough votes from Romero to cause his defeat.

There are many sources of Romero's views on statehood, for he has not hesitated to write or speak on his favorite subject. A very useful reference is his small (91-page) book called *La estadidad es para los pobres* (Statehood is for the Poor).[19] In this monograph, Romero makes a persuasive case for the thesis that those who would benefit most from statehood are those in Puerto Rican society most neglected at the present time: the young, the old, the poor, the unemployed, the homeless, in short, the disadvantaged.

In an article in *Foreign Affairs* titled "Puerto Rico, U.S.A., The Case for Statehood," Romero answers many of the arguments leveled against statehood.[20] He concludes:

"Our position is that throughout this century, in war and peace alike, we Puerto Ricans have demonstrated our loyalty to the principles of American democracy and to the private enterprise system, and that it is now high time we were granted the equality that our loyalty has earned, and to which our citizenship entitles us...

"We statehooders are therefore committed to forging a society in which, while remaining faithful to our linguistic and cultural traditions, we can make a full and meaningful contribution to building a better America, in exchange for full and meaningful participation in the process by which America is governed...

"The goal of the Puerto Rican people is political equality within a framework which will permit our island and our nation to prosper together. It is a goal which can and will be achieved."

In June 1983, Romero answered a series of questions on status in an interview with a reporter from the newspaper, *El Mundo*. The following question and answer is of particular interest in terms of Romero's inner motivation:

Question: "Are you a statehooder by conviction or by convenience?"

Answer: "I feel I am a statehooder by conviction. I am a statehooder because I believe in the principles of the American nation, and I believe in the democratic system of government. If I did not believe in this, I could not be a statehooder...

"We can be part of the nation and receive the benefits due us as a political community.

"Today we are part of the most coveted market in the world. We have access to and are a part of the nation, and these are things we would have to give up if we became independent. I have to look out for my people... We have to look out for the needy, those that have not had opportunities. How will the poor in our society be able to improve the education of their children, where will they be guaranteed the best hospital and medical services, under what system, under what relationship? I am not willing, just to be able to raise one flag and sing only one hymn, that the sons of my brothers live in hunger."[21]

Perhaps Romero's position is best summed up in a speech to the Puerto Rican Chamber of Commerce on August 17, 1983. He discusses at length the inadequacies and inequalities in relations with the United States:

1. lack of participation in federal decisions which affect Puerto Rico;
2. Supreme Court sanction of discrimination against U.S. citizens of Puerto Rico (Harris v. Rosario, 1980);
3. The fragile nature of the so-called "marginal benefits" of Commonwealth; and
4. Puerto Rico's position as last to receive benefits when they are dispensed but first to be cut in a budget reduction.

Puerto Rico will prosper, Romero said

1. "When we establish a political structure on the firm foundation of permanent union with the United States;
2. "When we acquire the rights of full participation in the benefits of citizenship... and
3. "When we occupy a position of relevance and respect within the federal power structure."

During the 1984 gubernatorial campaign, Romero hit hard at Commonwealth status. He said that Puerto Rico's relationship with the United States is one of "sharecropper" when it should be "co-owner" of the plantation. He accused the Popular Democratic Party of "selling out our political rights for presumed economic advantages." He said the real unity of purpose among Puerto Ricans can not be reached until the island stops being a "territory or colony" and chooses either statehood or independence.[22]

Initially, Romero had strong reservations about President Reagan's Caribbean Basin Initiative. In a 56-page report he submitted to The White House on December 17, 1981, he said that proposed U.S. tariff reductions on Caribbean products, especially rum, would have grave consequences on the Puerto Rican economy.[23] President Reagan took his report seriously and announced a series of adjustments to protect Puerto Rico. Chief of these was that Puerto Rico, along with the U.S. Virgin Islands, would receive the excise taxes levied by the federal government on Caribbean rum sold in the United States, to compensate for any losses they might incur due to such sales.

These measures were announced by Governor Romero the same day that President Reagan unveiled his Caribbean plan in a speech to the Organization of American States in Washington. Romero said that Puerto Rico would not be harmed and in fact would benefit in numerous ways from the CBI program.[24]

From that point on, Romero became a staunch supporter of the CBI and gave numerous speeches defending the plan against attacks from the opposition Popular Democratic Party at that time.[25]

One of the most controversial actions taken by Romero with respect to U.S.-Puerto Rican relations was his appearance before the United Nations Decolonization Committee in New York on August 28, 1978. Such action ran counter to U.S. policy of not giving prestige to this committee, whose jurisdiction over Puerto Rico the United States does not recognize. Furthermore, the United States was troubled with Romero's perception of Puerto Rico as a colony when the United Nations, itself, has taken Puerto Rico off its list of non-self governing territories.[26]

In his testimony, Romero presented himself, not as a plaintiff but as *amicus curae*. The political status of Puerto Rico, he said, is an internal matter, to be debated and resolved within Puerto Rico itself, in consultation with the United States, "the nation of which we are citizens. If, as is true, we (Puerto Ricans) have not yet reached a final decision, then the responsibility for our inaction lies with us and with us alone. We have the means to change our political status. Whether and how we shall use those means is for us and us alone to decide... I come before you today not to request that you intervene, but rather to explain why I believe you should not consider even attempting to intervene.

"I, myself, am on record to the effect that Puerto Rico's relationship with the United States retains vestiges of colonialism.

"Yet I do not come before you to solicit your intervention.

"Why?

"Because I believe such intervention can never be appropriate, relevant, or in the least bit effective until and unless it can be demonstrated that Puerto Rico lacks the wherewithal to freely determine its destiny."

Romero described the social and economic progress achieved under U.S. tutelage, lauded U.S. democratic achievements, and expressed confidence that the United States would respect the free will of the people of Puerto Rico with regard to a change in status, if and when such a change is ever requested. For the United Nations to try to impose on Puerto Rico a status it did not want would violate the principle of self-determination of peoples, Romero asserted.[27]

It was an eloquent presentation, but it did not move the committee, made up almost entirely of Soviet bloc and Third World nations. It proceeded to pass one of the strongest in a long series of resolutions condemning the United States, and called for the immediate transfer of all political power to Puerto Rico.[28]

On April 21, 1983, Romero vetoed a joint resolution of the Puerto Rican legislature asking for the U.S. Government to propose Puerto Rico as an associate member of UNESCO. In a lengthy speech on the subject to the Overseas Press Club of San Juan that same day, Romero outlined his reasons for the veto. His principal reason was that associate membership in the past has been given to colonies moving toward independence. He did not consider Puerto Rico in that category.[29]

With respect to Section 936 of the U.S. Internal Revenue Code, Romero has suggested that the only secure way to prolong its benefits for Puerto Rico for an extended period would be its inclusion in an Enabling Act for statehood for Puerto Rico, for a transitional period of 20 years.[30] He believes that statehood would provide greater economic security for Puerto Rico by guaranteeing to businessmen greater stability for their investments.[31]

On the cultural front, Romero believes that the language and culture of Puerto Rico can be safeguarded under statehood through guarantees written into its Enabling Act.[32]

As to security considerations, Romero sees Puerto Rico in a danger zone, under menace from Cuba and the Soviet Union. He rejects charges of militarization in Puerto Rico, saying that Puerto Rico, with its National Guard of less than 10,000, is one of the least militarized places on earth. "There are Russian ships in the area," he has said, "and I feel a lot better knowing there are American ships around to protect us."[33] He defended the Caribbean Basin Initiative in part on strategic grounds, as a way to stop the advance of communism in the region.[34]

Romero would use the following procedure to achieve statehood:

1. A plebiscite, Statehood yes or no.
2. If a majority of voters say yes, he would immediately file an Enabling Act.
3. Acceptance by the United States of three conditions: retention of Spanish as the official language of Puerto Rico; a 20-year transition period on the payment of federal taxes; and assumption by Congress of the island's public debt.

In 1981, on an NBC television program, Romero accepted a challenge by Hernández Colón to a Statehood, yes-or-no plebiscite, but Hernández Colón later reneged on the offer.

In late September 1986, Romero was designated by his party to fill a NPP seat in the Senate which suddenly became vacant. From this new platform, he has offered strong opposition to the Hernández-Colón Administration. He is opposed to a Constituent Assembly as the first step toward solving Puerto Rico's status problem, preferring instead a yes-or-no plebiscite on statehood or a plebiscite between statehood and independence. He favors full application of the proposed new federal minimum wage law to Puerto Rico. He has opposed the use of Puerto Rican Government funds for loans to Caribbean governments. He supports the use of Puerto Rican territories for U.S. military training, even the training of *Contra* forces. He favors the use of federal over state tribunals whenever possible. And he plans to challenge Governor Hernández for control of the Democratic Party of Puerto Rico.

Position of Luis A. Ferré

Known variously as Mr. Republican and Mr. Statehood of Puerto Rico, Luis A. Ferré, Chairman of the National Republican Party of Puerto Rico, founding president of the New Progressive Party, and a former Governor of Puerto Rico, now in his mid-80's has had a distinguished career in Puerto Rican politics and is listened to with considerable attention in both Puerto Rico and Washington, D.C.

Ferré was the inspiration behind a 1981 position paper that resulted in President Reagan's January 12, 1982 Declaration expressing his personal preference for statehood. Ferré's paper, co-authored with at-the-time San Juan Mayor Hernán Padilla and

Julia Rivera de Vincente, who was in charge of George Bush's winning presidential primary campaign in 1980 in Puerto Rico, asked Reagan to

1. Indicate his personal support for statehood and his hope that Puerto Rico will move swiftly and decisively in that direction;
2. Pledge that his administration will vigorously support statehood if it is formally petitioned by the people of Puerto Rico;
3. Agree to work with Puerto Rico for a smooth and mutually agreeable transition from Commonwealth status to statehood; and
4. Recognize that status is an issue to be solved solely by Puerto Rico and the United States and strongly discourage the United Nations and other countries from interfering in the issue.[35]

President Reagan's declaration touched on all of these points, and more, and was a triumph for Ferré and the New Progressive Party.

In a statement April 22, 1969 to the Puerto Rican region of the International Studies Association, Ferré, as new governor, set out his view on the role of Puerto Rico in Latin America and the Caribbean.

"Puerto Rico is not going to act as an independent state. Contrary to the practice of previous administrations, we are not going to interfere in the affairs of our Latin American neighbors. We will not act in the area except within the framework of U.S. foreign policy, helping in every possible way to make it understood as a policy of friendly cooperation and mutual respect.

"Let me tell you now of some of the things I think Puerto Rico can do. I think Puerto Rico can be a showcase of cooperation between U.S. capital and Latin American ingenuity. I think that Puerto Rico can act as a bridge between the Americas, as a catalyst in bringing the two cultures together. By our example, we can encourage other countries to undertake economic development and political and social reform. Because of our knowledge of the Spanish language and understanding of the Spanish culture, Puerto Rico can play a vital role in carrying out our nation's policy in Central and South America and the Caribbean.

We are in a privileged position to make friends for the United States by interpreting its culture and its true political and social objectives, which are often misunderstood.

"Our policy toward our Latin American neighbors will be one of friendship and cooperation. We will continue closer cultural cooperation, as in the annual trip of the Puerto Rican Symphony Orchestra. We will also seek closer trade relations and increase our interchange of products to the greatest extent possible. However, our principal trade will continue to be oriented toward the United States, where we already receive favorable economic concessions.

"There is a great deal that can and should be done with respect to closer cooperation in the Caribbean, and I will press President Nixon for more active participation by the Department of State and other federal agencies, using Puerto Rican personnel whenever possible.

"Our ties with the Dominican Republic, as our nearest Latin American neighbor, will always be close. You remember that the President of the Dominican Republic attended my inauguration, waving all his rights to protocol. Just last week, our Secretary of State and Secretary of Commerce visited Santo Domingo for Pan American Day celebrations and to initiate talks on closer commercial and tourist ties.

"We will continue to welcome and give a second home to refugees from Castro's tyranny. But we look forward to the day when there will be a change of regime in Cuba so that these persons can return to their homeland and enjoy there a democratic life of freedom and security."

In January 1982, Ferré led a high-level Puerto Rican Republican delegation to The White House which succeeded in persuading those working on President Reagan's Caribbean Basin Initiative to make some modifications to assure that Puerto Rico would not be harmed.[36]

He defended the initiative before a special committee of the Puerto Rican legislature and stated that the only way that Puerto Rico can achieve permanent union with the United States in conditions of dignity and economic security is through the equality of statehood.[37]

Ferré opened doors in Washington for Governor Hernández

Colón in joint lobbying for the preservation of Section 936 of the U.S. Internal Revenue Code. But Ferré pointed out that the U.S. Treasury was considering changes in the section precisely as "the result of the condition of political inferiority in which we find ourselves, which permits Congress and the [Reagan] administration to take unilateral actions on problems fundamental to Puerto Rico without giving us the right to express our points of view." He said:

"The only remedy under the American flag is to obtain political equality through statehood, which will give us political instruments through our congressmen and the presidential vote."[38]

When it appeared that the U.S. Treasury could not be deterred from its determination to eliminate this tax exemption program, Ferré suggested that Puerto Rico could gain substantial economic aid under the Appalachian Deprived Zone Investment Initiative program by becoming a state of the union.

According to Ferré, the economic benefits gained by the island as a deprived zone would be comparable to the benefits currently being received from Section 936. He pointed out that Tennessee, Kentucky, West Virginia and parts of New York were receiving aid under this program and said, "I have no doubt that Puerto Rico could also enjoy these benefits as a state."[39]

Ferré gave his blessing to Hernández Colón's trip to Japan in search of Japanese investments for Puerto Rico. "I am convinced that the initiative of trying to bring Japanese money to Puerto Rico is a good one."[40]

On July 17, 1986, Ferré made one of his rare appearances before a congressional committee in recent years when he testified before Congressman Morris Udall's Interior and Insular Affairs Committee on the subject of the role of the territories in international relations. His testimony was moderate in comparison with that of other members of his party who strongly attacked the Governor's initiatives abroad.

Ferré said:

"Since Commonwealth has not delivered its 'promised land,' and even though it is unlikely to deliver it, we have no other choice than to try to live with it as best we can until we reach statehood... Understandings are possible between Puerto Rico and other countries on issues pertinent to the economy... There should be nothing to stop Puerto Rico from seeking under-standings on cultural matters... The State Department, without in any way yielding its prerogatives, could choose to look the other way... If states can enter understandings, and if Puerto Rico is gradually moving toward statehood as a result of the failure of Commonwealth, I feel it most reasonable to enter into these types of linkages... But agreements and treaties, because of their bind-ing nature, are quite different from understandings. Puerto Rico can not move in this direction without an express mandate from our people..."

Ferré took issue with the proposed use of Section 936 funds deposited in Puerto Rican banks for loans in the Caribbean. This, he said, would evaluate 936 effectiveness in Puerto Rico on the basis of something divorced from its objective of creating jobs in Puerto Rico. He said:

"I think the 936 corporations and the Commonwealth do need time to re-think their strategy, especially since the former may come to the realization that a transition bill to statehood is the only real guarantee for their continued, but already limited, oper-ation.

"For example, the discretion of the Puerto Rican Develop-ment Bank in giving the loans to Governments and not to private enterprise is a foreign policy power. The possibility of favoring one nation over another, by whichever means we do it, is a foreign policy power. The possibility of preferential rates and preferential repayment schedules is a foreign policy power...

"What happens to a loan gone bad? How do we collect from another nation? From a company we might say we take over the collateral... What if we end up with a series of factories through-out the Caribbean?

"...these possibilities... are not the product of a consensus of our people, but they are likely the position of a group which supports only one status alternative. You'll never know the con-sensus unless you ask us: you can hold a fact-finding plebiscite in Puerto Rico... The Commonwealth has run its course... You can not patch it up. It needs replacement with a proven successful formula: statehood... It is time to have a new instrument, a fact-finding plebiscite, this time under the direction of Congress..."[41]

Ferré accompanied his testimony with a four-page statement entitled, "Statehood, a Question of Rights." He shows how, one by one, obstacles to statehood have been removed over the past 70 years, from the granting of U.S. citizenship in 1917 to the economic argument in more recent times. He concludes that "Puerto Rico will inevitably become a state of the union and will participate with greater significance in the resolution for human understanding which guides the American democratic experience."

Finally, it should be noted that Ferré does not agree with a Statehood, yes-or-no plebiscite, as advocated by nearly all other top NPP leaders. He said that "independence is a logical alternative to put before the voters. Commonwealth, though, is not realistic. It has no future."[42]

Position of other key leaders

Mayor Baltasar Corrada del Río and former Governors Carlos Romero Barceló and Luis A. Ferré are the most influential leaders of the New Progressive Party. Five legislators, however, deserve attention for the special interest they have taken in the status question: Senate Minority Leader Roberto Rexach Benítez; House Minority Leader José Granados Navedo; and Senators Miguel "Mickey" Miranda, Rolando Silva and Oreste Ramos.

Until recently, Rexach Benítez was a member of the Popular Democratic Party. "Until 1975," he said, "I believed that the Free Associated State could be culminated. But I am now convinced that it has no exit. The structure that would be necessary for its culmination does not fit the U.S. political or constitutional system. They are seeking all the powers of a republic without the responsibilities of a republic, and all the rights of a state without being a state. In terms of rights, this relationship would be more advantageous than the federal relationship of the states, and this is a political impossibility."[43]

In late 1985, when it became known that Puerto Rico's Resident Commissioner had quietly removed Puerto Rico from a bill to grant the presidential vote to the flag territories, Rexach Benítez and Senator Miranda introduced a resolution into the Puerto Rican Senate to have Puerto Rico restored to the bill.[44] But the

Popular Democratic Party in control of the Senate refused to act on the measure.

When, on January 14, 1986, a public opinion poll taken in Puerto Rico showed that 67% of the people of Puerto Rico (including 62% identifying with the Popular Democratic Party) wished to be able to vote for president and vice-president, Rexach Benítez and House Minority Leader José Granados simultaneously introduced bills in their respective houses calling for a plebiscite on the question in Puerto Rico.[45] Again, the Popular Democratic Party ignored the appeal.

Granados heads the *Comisión Estadista* (Statehood Commission), a dues-paying private organization dedicated to educating the people of Puerto Rico on statehood. The Commission holds monthly meetings, with speakers, and conducts courses and seminars on the status question.

Granados is in favor of calling a spade a spade. He objected strongly to the watering down of a party resolution in 1983 that substituted the words, "vestiges of colonialism," for the word, "colony," in describing Puerto Rico's relationship to the United States.[46]

In testimony to the House Interior and Insular Affairs Committee on April 10, 1986, Granados asked Congress to force a status plebiscite on Puerto Rico.

"We submit that the status quo lacks moral standing," he said, "since the 1967 plebiscite results that served as a moral basis for Commonwealth status 19 years ago are no longer valid. Since 1967, our electorate has doubled, from 1,067,349 voters to 2 million voters. Fully half of all voters today — all those under the age of 40 — were too young to vote in 1967. The 425,132 pro-Commonwealth votes whose plebiscite mandate to this day prop up the status quo represent less than 25% of our voters... "

"I suggest that it is time to tell the Puerto Rican Government to allow its people to freely express their status choice, not in the confusing morass of a general election, but in a separate plebiscite in which status is *the* issue... Give us the opportunity to take our case to the people... Congress can certainly force a vote in Puerto Rico... Let the people speak out."[47]

Senator Rolando Silva, National Democratic Committeeman of Puerto Rico, testified before Congress that "the problem of

Puerto Rico is colonialism, and decolonization stands at the eternal limelight of island politics... Congress must order and supervise a plebiscite to consult the U.S. citizens of Puerto Rico whether they want statehood or not... Is it your intention to keep us forever in this Twilight Zone or will you bring us out and let us join you as the 51st state of the union?"[48]

Statehood frustrations came to a climax on March 3, 1987 when a group of pro-statehood legislators, led by Senator Oreste Ramos, actually proposed "a state of civic rebellion" to force the United States to decolonize Puerto Rico.

The group proposed a "yes-or-no" plebiscite among the people of Puerto Rico as to their satisfaction with the status quo. Anticipating an overwhelming vote of dissatisfaction, they believe that a domestic and international crisis for the United States would be generated. A colony in rebellion would threaten the United States with independence if it did not take steps to resolve the crisis. Until a situation of crisis is created, Ramos said, the problem of status cannot be solved.

Ramos elaborated further on the idea in an article in *El Nuevo Día* March 10, 1987. The people of Puerto Rico, he wrote, "would demand American and international support for a change which conforms to the three decolonization alternatives recognized under international law: statehood, independence and the associated republic...

"When the federal powers realize that refusing to decolonize Puerto Rico may lead to the threat of independence... when they think about the possibility of losing the last naval bases remaining in the Caribbean, they will have no choice but to concede statehood."

In an interview in Ponce, Puerto Rico, March 22, 1987 Ramos said that in the event that the United States denied statehood to Puerto Rico, he proposed "to strike the colors of the American flag from La Fortaleza [the governor's mansion], fold them neatly and send them to the President of the United States, and to tell him that since this flag does not represent equality and democracy, there is no sense for it to be here."[49]

Positions of Puerto Ricans in Civic Action

The first grass roots citizens movement in the history of Puerto Rican politics was organized in 1984 to promote statehood for Puerto Rico.

It was the idea of a young housewife in Mayaguez, Puerto Rico, Dr. Miriam Ramírez de Ferrer, who was frustrated by the inability of political leaders to make progress on statehood. The chief problem, she felt, was that the status issue became entangled with party politics. She founded Puerto Ricans in Civic Action as a home for all people interested in achieving statehood, regardless of their political affiliation.

The group's principal activity has been the collection of individually signed petitions requesting statehood of the U.S. Congress. It has collected and delivered 250,000 such petitions to the Congress and intends to bring the total to a half million which is more than voted for Commonwealth in the 1967 plebiscite. When this goal is reached, the group expects that the President and Congress will honor their pledges to respect the freely-expressed will of the people of Puerto Rico with respect to their political future.

The group concentrates its activities on the promotion of statehood but also combats ideas to the detriment of statehood. For example, it exposed the fact that the Puerto Rican Resident Commissioner in the U.S. Congress removed Puerto Rico from the list of territories that would receive the presidential vote under H.J. 23 of January 3, 1985. It has documented activities of the Hernández Colón administration which the organization considers steps toward the formation of an associated republic leading to independence. On July 25, 1986, a small plane rented by the group flew over the Constitution Day celebration towing a banner, "Statehood yes, Republic no." On March 1, 1987, Puerto Ricans in Civic Action organized the celebration of 70 years of U.S. citizenship for the people of Puerto Rico. Over 1,000 persons attended. It was the largest pro-U.S. demonstration in 90 years of U.S.-Puerto Rican relations.

Dr. Ramírez has called for the incorporation of Section 936 of the U.S. Internal Revenue Code as a transitional provision in an Enabling Act, with its ultimate replacement with incentives compatible with statehood. She also lobbied hard for the re-insertion of Puerto Rico in H.J. 23 of January 3, 1985, which would have extended the presidential vote to the territories.

In testimony before the U.S. House Interior and Insular Affairs Committee on May 22, 1986, Dr. Ramírez cited the following as benefits that would flow to the United States and Puerto Rico from Puerto Rican statehood:

"Statehood for Puerto Rico would culminate our political evaluation and earn new respect for the United States in the Caribbean and Latin America.

"With statehood, U.S. relations with Puerto Rico would be placed on a more orderly and predictable basis than under the undefined Commonwealth.

"As a state, Puerto Rico would provide a stable, secure and reliable base for the defense of our nation in the Caribbean;

"For Puerto Rico, statehood would also mean an increase in financial investments because of the stable political situation found in full-fledged states.

"Intellectual efforts in Puerto Rico would be focused on productive areas instead of sterile debates about status.

"Our tourism industry would prosper as the rest of the nation accepts Puerto Rico in its fold, as happened in Hawaii."

Position of the United States

The basic U.S. position on statehood, as with free association and independence, is that any initiative for change must come from Puerto Rico, and that the United States will respect the will of the Puerto Rican people. While adhering to this official position, both President Reagan and Vice President Bush have expressed strong personal preferences for statehood and have lent support and encouragement to the statehood movement.

As candidate for President in 1980, Ronald Reagan issued a strong call for Puerto Rican statehood in a long article in *The Wall Street Journal*. Following are some salient excerpts:[50]

"When I formally announced my intention to seek the Republican presidential nomination in 1980, my televised speech to the nation included a commitment to not only support statehood for Puerto Rico if the people of the island Commonwealth desire statehood. It also included a commitment that, as President, I would initiate statehood legislation, which really means that I

99

would take the lead in persuading the people of Puerto Rico — the mainland United States — all American citizens — that statehood will be good for all of us...

"...the pivot of the struggle is among our fellow citizens in the Puerto Rican Commonwealth...

"Our keen 'peacefully co-existing' competitor, the Soviet Union, is not unaware of the importance of Puerto Rico in the great global contest of ideas. As a 'Commonwealth,' Puerto Rico is now neither a state nor independent, and thereby has an historically unnatural status. There is this raw nerve to rub, and our Marxist-Leninist competitors rub it... We can't merely defend ourselves against this attack. We must ourselves attack, not with terror but with statehood.

"It is as simple as this: If we in the United States can not design a model for a political economy that is sufficiently attractive, if we can not win over our fellow citizens in Puerto Rico to the nuptials that statehood involves, how can our model succeed as an instrument of foreign policy anywhere in the world?

"To show the world that the American idea can work in Puerto Rico is to show that our idea can work anywhere."

As President, and at the request of former Governor Luis A. Ferré and other statehood leaders, Reagan issued the following declaration on January 12, 1982:

"When I announced my candidacy for this office more than two years ago, I pledged to support statehood for the Commonwealth of Puerto Rico, should the people of that island choose it in a free and democratic election. Today, I reaffirm that support, still confident in my belief that statehood would benefit both the people of Puerto Rico and their fellow American citizens in the 50 states.

"While I believe the Congress and the people of this country would welcome Puerto Rico statehood, this Administration will accept whatever choice is made by a majority of the island's population.

"No nation, no organization, nor individual should mistake our intent in this. The status of Puerto Rico is an issue to be settled by the peoples of Puerto Rico and the United States. There must be no interference in the democratic process.

"Puerto Ricans have borne the responsibilities of U.S. citizenship with honor and courage for more than 64 years. They have fought beside us for decades and have worked beside us for generations. Puerto Rico is playing an important role in the development of the Caribbean Basin Initiative, and its strong tradition of democracy provides leadership and stability in that region. In statehood, the language and culture of that island — rich in history and tradition — would be respected, for in the United States the cultures of the world live together with pride.

"We recognize the right of the Puerto Rican people to self determination. If they choose statehood, we will work together to devise a union of promise and opportunity in our federal union of sovereign states."

On subsequent occasions, when questioned about his views on the status of Puerto Rico, the President has authorized White House officials to reaffirm this position. Typical of such reaffirmation is a letter dated April 2, 1985, from presidential assistant Ronald L. Alvarado to former Governor Ferré certifying that President Reagan "fully supports and encourages statehood for the island and would eagerly welcome Puerto Rico into the union as the 51st state."[51]

George Bush, as candidate for the presidential nomination and as Vice President, has been even more effusive. In the 1980 presidential primary in Puerto Rico, he campaigned with the slogan, "Statehood Now," winning the primary and taking an early lead for the nomination.

Vice President Bush personally received about 100 members of Puerto Ricans in Civic Action at The White House on June 18, 1985, on the occasion of their delivery of 100,000 statehood petitions to Washington. Following are excerpts of remarks made by him on that occasion:

"It gives me great pleasure to join you here in the Indian Treaty Room to celebrate this 'down payment' of 100,000 signatures supporting statehood for the Commonwealth of Puerto Rico.

"I see among you so many personal friends. Miguel García Méndez, whose wisdom I have drawn on for years and whose dedication to the Republican Party is exceeded only by his extraordinary concern for all humanity.

"And, of course, I have to say what a tonic it is to see Julia

Rivera de Vincenti, who was my wonderful campaign chairman during the 1980 presidential primary in Puerto Rico.

"And, finally, I must mention my dear friend, Miriam Ferrer, founder and until recently President of the Puerto Rican Federation of Republican Women and Republican National Committeewoman from Puerto Rico. Now, she has put partisanship aside and devotes virtually all her time and remarkable talents to gain statehood for Puerto Rico.

"In a free country, one person can help others to believe in themselves and the rightness of their cause. Miriam Ferrer is such a person, and she inspires others like her to pursue their dreams.

"Your presence here today, your achievement of 100,000 signatures, and your resolve to persuade your fellow citizens to support statehood: all these things are testimony to what is possible when one individual — and one team of individuals — really care.

"President Reagan and I believe strongly that if Puerto Rico's three million citizens want statehood, Puerto Rico should be admitted as the 51st state of the union.

"I know that when the people of Puerto Rico participate fully in the political and economic institutions of the United States, they will bring a vigorous, fresh, and informed perspective to our public councils.

"I also know what Puerto Rico is a window of the Caribbean through which the people of the South may look at our nation's democratic ways and notice that we do, indeed, practice what we believe.

"We believe in the good sense of the people. We believe in the rule of law and the dignity of the individual. We believe that government should be limited in its powers and that individuals should be free to say what they think and think what their consciences and common sense dictate.

"These are remarkable principles, inspiring in their statement and significant in their practice.

"So, if the people of Puerto Rico choose statehood, I guarantee that this Administration will work with Congress to admit Puerto Rico to the union.

"I commend your effort and your achievement thus far. Best

wishes in gaining your goals. I have enjoyed being here with you."

At a private reception at the Caribe Hilton Hotel in San Juan September 21, 1985, Vice President Bush told statehooders: "We're ready when you are. Contrary to some reports, this Administration is totally committed to statehood for Puerto Rico as soon as it can be proven to be the desire of a majority of its citizens."

Ferré asked Bush for comment on a column which appeared in *El Nuevo Día* predicting that Puerto Rico will be a republic on October 12, 1992, the 500th anniversary of the discovery of the New World by Christopher Columbus. In a letter written "en route to China, October 11, 1985" the Vice President replied:

"Dear Don Luis:

"I read that column you sent me with its absurd conclusion. I have been and always will favor statehood. I will repeat here what I have constantly said. Statehood now! That's *my* position. I have always recognized the right of people to choose the form of government they want.

"My respects and best wishes. Always (signed) George Bush"[52]

In a video-tape message to a hemispheric conference of mayors in San Juan in June, 1986 the Vice President stated:

"President Reagan and I share your concerns and we are ready to work with you in the search for new ways to confront these challenges.

"To do this, we must have mutual respect and profound understanding of the patriotism and the cultural diversity of the Americas. And we must also recognize our common goals and interests.

"Puerto Rico is a magnificent example. Her rich cultural patronage has been maintained in the last 89 years of her relations with the United States, and I am one who wants to see Puerto Rico convert herself into the 51st state of the United States of America."[53] The message was well received by the hemisphere's mayors.

On April 13, 1987, Vice President Bush reiterated his support for Puerto Rican statehood following a meeting with Puerto Rican political and business leaders. His message reflected the impact that delivery of petitions by Puerto Ricans in Civic Action was having on White House thinking with respect to statehood. Bush said, "The hundreds of thousands of Puerto Rican people who have petitioned Congress for statehood recognition deserve to be heard on Capitol Hill. If the people of Puerto Rico want statehood, we should be everything we can to facilitate the admission of Puerto Rico as the 51st State of the union. Statehood will permit the people of Puerto Rico, who take their U.S. citizenship very seriously and have contributed much to this country, to fully participate in our great democracy. "[54]

On May 16, 1967, Bush said that as President he would (1) issue an executive order replacing a Kennedy memorandum so that Puerto Rico will be treated as much as possible like a state and continue to maintain a relationship with the executive branch of government with a direct line of communication to the Office of the President; (2) initiate legislation before congress that would "incorporate" Puerto Rico, so that it would be in a position similar to other entities that became states; (3) appoint a task force made up of people from Puerto Rico and the mainland to prepare enabling legislation that includes a plan for economic transition and is sensitive to the cultural identity of Puerto Rico; (4) initiate legislation that insures that the people of Puerto Rico have the opportunity to have a referendum on the statehood question irrespective of the party in power in Puerto Rico; and (5) as soon as the people approve statehood, forward a statehood bill to Congress. He believes that at that point, statehood can not be denied.[55]

On May 12, 1987, Senate Minority Leader Robert Dole introduced a bill "to provide for a referendum in Puerto Rico on the admission of Puerto Rico into the Union as a State." Senator Paul Simon (D.-Ill.), an announced candidate for the 1988 presidential nomination, is a co-sponsor of the bill, along with Senator Spark M. Matsunaga (D.-Hawaii) and Senator Alfonse M. D'Amato (R.-N.Y.). The bill, which was referred to the Senate Energy and Natural Resources Committee (which handles territorial matters), reads as follows:

"Be it enacted by the Senate and House of Representatives of the United Sates of America in Congress assembled, Section 1. Findings.

"The Congress finds that —

(1) States have been admitted to the Union only after residents of the proposed States have requested statehood;

(2) residents of Puerto Rico have been given only one opportunity, in 1967, to determine for themselves whether they wish to be admitted to the Union as a State, and

(3) as citizens of the United States, residents of Puerto Rico should be allowed to express themselves once again on being admitted to the Union.

Sec. 2. Referendum.

"(a) Upon the call of the Governor of Puerto Rico, an islandwide referendum shall be held in Puerto Rico in order to enable the qualified voters of the Commonwealth of Puerto Rico to vote for admission of Puerto Rico into the Union. The referendum shall occur no earlier than January 1, 1989, and not later than December 31, 1994. In the referendum the qualified electors of the Commonwealth of Puerto Rico shall vote for the adoption or rejection of the following proposition, 'Shall Puerto Rico be admitted into the Union as a State?' ".

"(b) The returns of the referendum held under this Act shall be made to the Governor of Puerto Rico, who shall cause them to be canvassed in the manner provided by law for the canvass of votes cast in general elections in the Commonwealth of Puerto Rico. If a majority of the qualified voters voting in a referendum under this Act vote in favor of admission into the Union, the Governor shall certify to the President and the Congress of the United States the decision of the people of Puerto Rico.

"(c) The election laws of the Commonwealth of Puerto Rico shall apply to the referendum under this Act. The Governor of Puerto Rico shall prescribe such regulations governing the conduct of the referendum under this Act as may be necessary to supplement such laws in order to carry out this Act.

Sec. 3 Authorization of appropriations.

"There are hereby authorized to be appropriated such sums as may be necessary for defraying the direct costs of conducting the referendum provided for in this Act."[56]

Congressman Jack Kemp (R.-N.Y.), another presidential aspirant, was asked at the 1984 Republican National Convention if he endorsed statehood for Puerto Rico. His immediate answer was, "Yes, you bet." Then he added, "It should be self-determination, and if they decide in a vote to opt for statehood, I'm all for it."[57]

Congressman Robert J. Lagomarsino (R.-Cal.) a ranking member of the House Interior and Insular Affairs Committee, has been a strong ally of Puerto Ricans in Civic Action in their quest for statehood. He sent his chief aide, Manase Mansur, to the municipality of San Juan's 1986 Independence Day observance with a message that made clear his strong conviction that Puerto Rico should be admitted as the 51st state of the union. On March 5, 1987, he praised in Congress the work of Dr. Miriam Ramírez de Ferrer, President of Puerto Ricans in Civic Action, in organizing, on March 1, 1987, the celebration of the 70th anniversary of the granting of U.S. citizenship to the people of Puerto Rico.[58]

An area of conflict exists between most proponents of statehood in Puerto Rico and most political leaders in the United States with respect to the essential nature of the U.S.-Puerto Rican relationship. Most Puerto Rican advocates of statehood view Puerto Rico's status as colonial, or at least as having vestiges of colonialism, because of the island's position of political inferiority in comparison to the position of the 50 states of the union.

The term "colonialism" grates on U.S. sensitivities because this view is similar to accusations hurled against the United States by its worst enemies. The official position of the United States is that Puerto Rico is not a colony and cites as proof the fact that the United Nations removed Puerto Rico from its list of non-self-governing territories in 1953 under UNGA Resolution 748 (VIII).

If the United States were to admit that Puerto Rico is a colony, it would undermine objections by the United States to re-examination of U.S.-Puerto Rican relations by the international body.

It is a question of semantics, but nevertheless a question with deep political connotations. This unnecessary point of tension in U.S.-Puerto Rican relations can be avoided if those in Puerto Rico who want a change in the U.S.-Puerto Rican relationship would assume the more positive position of wanting to culminate

Commonwealth. Each of the status options can be viewed as a culmination of Commonwealth, albeit in different ways.

Possibly the most insightful observations on the U.S. position with respect to statehood were made by Andrew H. Card, Jr., Special Assistant to the President for Intergovernmental Affairs. Card suggested that it might be more productive to examine U.S. actions rather than words in assessing official U.S. feelings on the status of Puerto Rico. He made the following comment to the author in an interview in his office on April 10, 1986:

"You will notice that the point of responsibility for Puerto Rico within the Executive Branch of the U.S. Government is not the Department of the Interior, which handles U.S. relations with the territories, nor the Department of State, which handles U.S. relations with sovereign states. It is here in the Office of Inter-governmental Affairs at The White House, which handles federal relations with the states of the union. This has been the case under both the Carter and Reagan administrations. This, I think, tells us something about U.S. thinking on Puerto Rico."

Statehood Prospects

In evaluating requests for statehood, the U.S. Congress has been guided by three admission criteria:

"(1) That the inhabitants of the proposed new state are imbued with and sympathetic toward the principles of democracy, as exemplified in the American form of government;

"(2) That a majority of the electorate desire statehood; and

"(3) That the proposed state has sufficient population and resources to support a state government and to provide its share of the cost of the federal government."[59]

Puerto Rico fulfills the first of these criteria. Its constitution is modeled after that of the United States, and a vibrant democracy has functioned since the founding of the Commonwealth government in 1952. But Puerto Rico has yet to demonstrate that the majority of the electorate desire statehood, and it is unlikely that Congress would be impressed by a bare majority.[60] The island fulfills the population requirement of the third criterion, but there is some question as to the island's capacity to support both a state government and a fair share of the cost of the federal government. This might be possible if the 20-year transition period proposed by statehood advocates is authorized by the Congress and generous transition measures are allowed.

Thus, if a significant majority of the people of Puerto Rico should express themselves in favor of statehood in a plebiscite, Congress would undoubtedly focus on transitional arrangements. That body might find a request for a 20-year transition period to be excessive. Using Alaska as an example,[61] the Alaska Omnibus Act of 1959 provided transition grants for a five-year period. Following an earthquake in 1964, the act was amended to provide for additional transitional aid. Finally, the Alaska Native Claims Settlement Act, passed in 1971, twelve years after the admission of Alaska as a state of the union, granted nearly $1 billion to the new state.[62]

However, it should be observed that the nation's economic situation has changed drastically since the time that Alaska and Hawaii were admitted to the union. In 1959, and indeed through the 1960s and early 70s, the United States could afford the kind of generosity that it bestowed on these two territories. Since then, the nation has gone through a couple of recessions. The mood in Congress is toward belt-tightening, as reflected in the Gramm-Rudman-Hollings requirement. There is greater reluctance in Congress today to take on new economic burdens.

It might be more realistic for statehooders to request a transitional period of 10 years, realizing that, in all probability, transitional aid would be extended for a longer period if hardships were encountered. Congress would probably require Puerto Rico to make a more concerted effort to arrive at an equal footing with the other 50 states than 20 years would imply. This might imply a major reorientation of economic policy, from state socialism to greater economic freedom. But the transition to statehood would be no more difficult than the transition to independence, for which independence advocates are asking only 10 years. In most respects, Puerto Rico is already being treated as a state by the Federal Government. And, in the final analysis, Congress has never permitted a new state to go bankrupt.

A major area of controversy between statehood advocates and U.S. policy makers has to do with language. All advocates of statehood insist that Spanish be maintained as the official language of Puerto Rico. On the other hand, U.S. official opinion runs the gamut from those who would flatly oppose the admission of a Spanish-speaking state to the union to those willing to accept both Spanish and English as official languages in Puerto Rico.

These two positions are reflected in supplemental views of Senators Henry M. Jackson and Jacob K. Javits in the 1966 Report of the United States-Puerto Rico Commission on the Status of Puerto Rico.[63]

Senator Jackson wrote: "The people of Puerto Rico represent an old and rich culture. We welcome diversity; therefore, the distinctive culture of Puerto Rico presents no bar as such to Statehood. The unity of our Federal-State structure, however, requires a common tongue. We do not have to look far to see what has happened in certain countries that have failed to adhere to this fundamental practice. Surely, at a time when we are trying to eliminate ghettos of all kinds, we should not establish within our Federal-State system a language ghetto. A condition precedent to Statehood must be the recognition and acceptance of English as the official language. The continuance of Spanish as a second language would not be inconsistent with this requirement."

Senator Javits wrote: "With regard to the language question relating to Statehood, I wish to underscore the Commission's view that while Statehood would necessarily involve a language accommodation to the rest of the United States, the Commission does not see this as an insurmountable barrier; nor need this require the surrender of the Spanish language.

"The question of an official language, or languages, will, of course, arise and require settlement at the time Statehood is established. But there is no need for the Commission to settle that question now, nor is there any reason to believe that this will become a difficult problem at the time of Statehood. The bilingual capability in Puerto Rico is growing at such a rate as to minimize its importance as time goes on. Further, there is ample evidence for the designation of two official languages in Puerto Rico, should this be desirable.

"Those who have raised concern over such an eventuality overlook the fact that there are over 20 countries today which have at least two official languages and where such a system is working resoundingly well — including such nations as Belgium, India, Pakistan, Israel, Czechoslovakia, Laos, Afghanistan and

Finland. Switzerland provides the best example of linguistic harmony with three official languages (French, German, Italian, and fourth, Rhaeto-Romanic, as a 'national language.') Only Canada, which has had a dual language system since 1867, has encountered any problems of note, and in this case, language difficulties were symptomatic, rather than the cause, of the differences between French-speaking Quebec and the rest of Canada. The experience and spirit of our own Nation, in welcoming and accommodating diversity of all peoples, is much more pertinent as an augury that two official languages in Puerto Rico would, if need be, turn out well."

Actually, a statute passed in Puerto Rico in 1902 establishes both English and Spanish as the official languages of the island. A tacit agreement to leave well enough alone might be the best compromise on this issue.

Ironically, what could be most helpful to statehood would be an eventuality that the United States has fought against with all its diplomatic power over the past 15 years — condemnation of the present relationship as colonial by the UN General Assembly. In practical terms, this would force a choice in Puerto Rico between statehood and independence. At this point in time, the results would probably run about 80 percent for statehood and 20 percent for independence.

NOTES
Chapter III

1. Platform of the New Progressive Party, 1984.

2. p. 10, *The San Juan Star*, May 13, 1983.

3. *Programa de Gobierno Propuesto por el Nuevo Partido Progresista para 1985-89*. Available from the headquarters of the New Progressive Party in Santurce, Puerto Rico.

4. p. 3, *El Nuevo Día*, January 15, 1985.

5. p. 8, *El Nuevo Día*, July 18, 1986 and p. 1, *The San Juan Star*, July 18, 1986.

6. Statement by The Honorable Baltasar Corrada del Río, Mayor of the Capital City of San Juan, Puerto Rico, before the House Committee on Interior and Insular Affairs, July 17, 1986.

7. p. 12-A, *El Mundo*, April 29, 1982.

8. Reprinted on p. 2, Outlook Section, *The San Juan Star*, June 27, 1982.

9. pp. E-1 and 8-A, *El Mundo*, November 29, 1984.

10. p. 5, *El Nuevo Día*, March 27, 1985.

11. p. 3, *The San Juan Star*, March 27, 1985.

12. p. 10, *El Nuevo Día*, June 15, 1986; p. 3, *The San Juan Star*, June 16, 1986.

13. p. 56, *El Nuevo Día*, July 2, 1986; p. 9, *El Nuevo Día*, July 13, 1986; p. 4, *El Mundo*, July 18, 1986; p. 13, *El Mundo*, July 22, 1986; p. 3, *The San Juan Star*, July 2, 1986.

14. p. 34, *The San Juan Star*, June 28, 1984; p. 15-A, *El Mundo*, July 2, 1984; p. 3-A, *El Mundo*, June 13, 1984.

15. p. 10, *The San Juan Star*, March 14, 1985; p. 4, *El Mundo*, March 14, 1985.

16. p. 13, *The San Juan Star*, p. 6, *El Mundo*, and p. 9, *El Nuevo Día*, July 22, 1985.

17. p. 2-A, *El Mundo*, December 3, 1981.

18. p. 14, *El Nuevo Día*, October 21, 1985.

19. First edition, November 18, 1973. Second edition, June 30, 1974. Page 17 of the August 13, 1974 issue of *The San Juan Star* carries a summary of its contents.

20. *Foreign Affairs*, Vol. 59, No. 1, Fall 1980, pp. 60-81.

21. p. 10-A, *El Mundo*, June 19, 1983.

22. p. 3, *The San Juan Star*, April 25, 1984.

23. p. 10, *El Nuevo Día*, January 26, 1982.

24. p. 1, *The San Juan Star*, February 25, 1982.

25. p. 56, *El Nuevo Día*, p. 20, *The San Juan Star*, p. 11-C, *El Mundo*, April 2, 1982; p. 6-A, *El Mundo* and p. 128, *El Nuevo Día*, December 1, 1983.

26. UNGA Res. 748 (1953).

27. For full text in Spanish, see p. 12-A, *El Mundo*, August 19, 1978.

28. UN document A/33/23 Rev. 1. 1, September 12, 1978.

29. p. 3, *The San Juan Star*, April 22, 1983.

30. p. 1 and 6-B, *El Mundo*, December 10, 1984.

31. p. 3, *El Nuevo Día*, July 1, 1984.

32. p. 5, *El Nuevo Día*, December 4, 1981.

33. p. 24, *El Nuevo Día*, p. 5, *The San Juan Star*, May 13, 1984.

34. p. 25, *El Nuevo Día*, p. 7-B, *El Mundo*, June 7, 1982.

35. p. 6, *The San Juan Star*, March 12, 1981.

36. p. 4, *El Nuevo Día*, December 15, 1982.

37. p. 16-A, *El Mundo*, March 18, 1982.

38. p. 3, *The San Juan Star*, March 12, 1985; p. 1, *The San Juan Star*, March 13, 1985; p. 8, *El Nuevo Día*, December 18, 1985.

39. p. 3, *The San Juan Star*, April 15, 1985.

40. p. 3, *The San Juan Star*, November 28, 1985.

41. Statement by Luis A. Ferré before the Committee on Interior and Insular Affairs, U.S. House of Representatives, July 17, 1986.

42. p. 2, *The San Juan Star*, September 14, 1984.

43. p. 4, *El Mundo*, July 21, 1986.

44. p. 14, *El Nuevo Día*, November 14, 1985.

45. p. 2, *The San Juan Star*, January 14, 1986.

46. pp. 2, 3, and 4, *Adelante*, Vol. 2, No. 23, San Juan, P.R. May 1983.

47. Testimony of the Honorable José Granados Navedo before the Committee on Interior and Insular Affairs, U.S. House of Representatives, April 10, 1986.

48. Testimony of the Honorable Rolando Silva before the Committee on Interior and Insular Affairs, U.S. House of Representatives, Washington, D.C., April 10, 1986.

49. The "Ramos rebellion" is reported on page 5 of *El Mundo*, March 4, 1987; Ramos's article on page 43 of *El Nuevo Día*, March 10, 1987; and the Ponce interview on page 10 of *El Nuevo Día*, March 22, 1987.

50. *Wall Street Journal*, February 11, 1980.

51. p. 3. *The San Juan Star*, April 15, 1985.

52. A photostat of this letter appears on p. 51, *El Nuevo Día*, November 27, 1985.

53. p. 19, *El Nuevo Día*; p. 24, *El Mundo*, June 19, 1985 and p. 53, *El Nuevo Día*, July 9, 1986.

54. Press release, Office of the Vice President, The White House, Washington, D.C., April 13, 1987.

55. Statement by the George Bush for President committee, San Juan, Puerto Rico, May 16, 1987.

56. S. 1182, 100th Congress, First Session, May 13, 1987.

57. Transcript from interview with Congressman Jack Kemp (R.-N.Y.) by Christopher Crommett, August 24, 1984, on the Republican Convention floor, Dallas, Texas.

58. Congressional Record, 100th Congress, First Session, Vol. 133, No. 34, March 5, 1987. On June 30, 1987, Congressman Lagomarsino introduced a pro-statehood bill in the U.S. House of Representatives.

59. General Accounting Office, Report to Congress, GGD-81-48, Government Printing Office, Washington, D.C., March 2, 1981, p.4, quoted from the Senate report that accompanied the latest admission act.

60. The lowest majority percentage which impelled a state to initiate the admission process was 58.5 percent in Alaska's first statehood plebiscite in 1946. But Alaska's official petition languished in congressional committee. In 1955, 61.1 percent of the voters approved the use of the Tennessee plan for admission to the union; 38.8 percent were opposed. This resulted in an Admission Act, which was approved in 1958 by 83.5 percent of the Alaskan voters. See *The American Statehood Process and Its Relevance to Puerto Rico's Colonial Reality: An Historical and Constitutional Perspective*, by Nelida-Jiménez Vásquez and Luis R. Dávila-Colón, Editorial Universitaria, University of Puerto Rico, Río Piedras, Puerto Rico, 1984.

61. Alaska is a good example for comparison to Puerto Rico because the territory was in dire financial straits when statehood was granted. On the other hand, Hawaii, the last state to be admitted to the union, was blessed with a vigorously growing economy and had few transition problems.

62. General Accounting Office, *Report to the Congress*, GGD-80-26, U.S. Government Printing Office, Washington, D.C., March 7, 1980, pp. 28-32.

63. U.S. Government Printing Office, Washington, D.C., August 1966, pp. 22 and 23.

Chapter IV

THE INDEPENDENCE OPTION AND ITS PROSPECTS

The independence movement in Puerto Rico is divided into two principal components: the Puerto Rican Independence Party (PIP), which adheres to the social democratic political ideology, and the Puerto Rican Socialist Party (PSP), which is marxist. The latter is a political movement rather than a political party. It last contested an election in 1976 and lost its official standing under the electoral law of Puerto Rico when it failed to receive 5 percent of the vote for Governor in that election. It achieved only .6 percent of that vote, and it never sought to re-register. The Puerto Rican Independence Party regularly participates in island elections. It received less than 4 percent of the vote for Governor in the 1984 election but maintained its official status through the election of two members of the legislature.

The PIP and PSP generally coincide in their interpretations of Puerto Rico's status, past and present, but they differ radically on the tactics and strategy by which changes in status should be made. They both see Puerto Rico as a colony under the control of the United States, exploited not only in the economic but also in the political and cultural sense. They both consider establishment of a national identity as their first order of business. Accordingly, their goals are clear: disposal of the territory of Puerto Rico by the U.S. Congress through the transfer of full power to the people of Puerto Rico.

Both the PIP and the PSP emphasize the benefits of nationhood and national sovereignty — the right under international law to complete and exclusive control of one's internal and external affairs without outside interference. They feel that statehood would be tantamount to national suicide. Puerto Rico, they say, would be swallowed up by the U.S. giant and lose its cultural and national identity. They stress the dignity of being master of one's house and the right to control one's destiny and natural resources. They feel that the only way for the island to become economically viable is to break out of its dependency syndrome and to liberate the creative spirit of its people.

Beyond this, however, the PIP and PSP diverge considerably with respect to basic doctrine, tactics and strategy. They are considered separately so that such distinctions may be better understood and appreciated.

Position of the Puerto Rican Independence Party (PIP)[1]

The PIP agrees with the pro-statehood New Progressive Party (PNP) that Puerto Rico is a colony of the United States and that a change of status is a prerequisite to the correction of the country's basic economic and social ills. But the two parties take opposite positions as to the direction such change should take.

Whereas the NPP sees statehood as the best escape from colonialism, the PIP feels that integration of Puerto Rico into the U.S. federal union would destroy the island's separate national identity and considers an independent, sovereign republic as the only dignified way to decolonize.

The PIP decries the excessive dependence of the island on the United States, for external aid, for investment capital, for social benefits, for consumer-oriented products and many other items. It wishes to free Puerto Rico from such dependence through control of its own resources. For example, the PIP asserts that Puerto Rico as an independent nation could claim control of 200 nautical miles of its off-shore waters, instead of the 12 miles permitted to the Commonwealth under its present political status.

The party's position with respect to the basic constitutional relationship between Puerto Rico and the United States is simple: transformation of that relationship to one between two sovereign states. Puerto Rico would have its own national flag, hymn and sports identity. Federal agencies would be withdrawn from the island, and relations between the two nations would be conducted through a U.S. Embassy in Puerto Rico and a Puerto Rican Embassy in Washington. The rules of international law would apply. Puerto Rico would set its own tariffs, minimum wage and immigration quotas. It would make, administer and interpret its own laws. It would coin its own money and establish its own monetary, industrial, tourism, commercial and other policies. Puerto Rico would have its own citizenship. It would negotiate its own treaties and other international agreements, participate as a full member of international organizations, provide for its own security, establish its own maritime policy and otherwise enjoy all the attributes of a sovereign state. U.S. Social Security payments would continue to Puerto Rican citizens now receiving them, but all monies paid into the system by Puerto Ricans not yet eligible for social security benefits would be transferred to Puerto Rico's own social security system.

The party accepts U.S. citizenship for the time being as a political necessity under present circumstances but feels that it was something imposed upon the Puerto Rican nation against its will in 1917 to justify drafting Puerto Ricans for military service during World War I. With the conversion of Puerto Rico into an independent republic, the people of Puerto Rico will form a new nation state with a citizenship of its own, which will be recognized and respected throughout the world. This, not free association nor statehood, the PIP contends, spells equality and dignity.

The 1984 PIP political party platform reveals in considerable detail the intentions of the new sovereign government, if and when independence is achieved. U.S. citizens born in Puerto Rico, or of Puerto Rican parents residing in Puerto Rico at the time the new republic is proclaimed, would acquire an international Puerto Rican citizenship. Anyone born in Puerto Rico who wished to conserve his or her U.S. citizenship would be obliged to so inform the U.S. Embassy in Puerto Rico. They would convert to resident aliens. U.S. citizens not born in Puerto Rico could acquire Puerto Rican citizenship through naturalization. The United States would be asked to establish a special immigration quota for Puerto Ricans for a period of ten years following independence.

If it should come to power, the PIP would petition at once for independence and request a ten-year transition period for the purpose of adjusting to the new status. To compensate for "past exploitation" by the United States, the PIP will ask for an indemnification by the U.S. Government over a ten-year period in the form of contributions to a special Development and Economic Reconstruction Fund, as part of the U.S. foreign aid program.

The PIP has also suggested that all U.S. property in Puerto Rico be turned over to the new nation at the time of its birth. The U.S. Government owns 91,351 acres of land in Puerto Rico, as well as millions of dollars of movable and immovable property.

The Puerto Rican Independence Party has worked through various international bodies, especially the Permanent Conference of Latin American Political Parties, the Socialist International and the United Nations in the quest for the Puerto Rican independence.

The Puerto Rican Independence Party is unalterably opposed to direct participation by Puerto Rico in the politics of the United States, viewing such participation as a step toward assimilation of the Puerto Rican nation into the American nation. However, the party has enlisted individual Congressmen to support their cause. Representative Ronald Dellums, a Democratic congressmen from California, has introduced a bill for Puerto Rican independence into each session of Congress.

In 1985, PIP's two elected representatives to the state legislature chose to take their oath of office separately from other elected legislators. After swearing to defend the Constitutions of the United States and Puerto Rico against all enemies, foreign and domestic, they declared that "this oath should be understood in the context of our supreme commitment to the struggle for independence of Puerto Rico and what this implies."[2]

The party, however, has so far adhered to the democratic process and has publicly condemned the use of violence as an instrument in the struggle for independence. Indeed, the PIP is currently seeking to project itself as the vehicle for democratic consensus for the solution of Puerto Rico's status dilemma, regardless of what the ultimate choice might be.[3]

The leading spokesman for the PIP is Rubén Berríos, the party's president and only representative in the Senate. Two other leading figures are Fernando Martín, vice president of the party and its unsuccessful candidate for governor in 1984, and David Noriega, the party's only member of the Puerto Rican House of Representatives.

Because of the smallness of the party and its high level of discipline, the views expressed by any of these three generally coincide with and can be considered to reflect the party's official position.

Position of Rubén Berríos Martínez

Rubén Berríos is an intellectual with his feet on the ground. He is a rare combination of successful academic and effective politician. He has ably blended teaching with a career in politics. A state senator and president of his party, he is also a distinguished professor of law at the University of Puerto Rico. He is dynamic, articulate, intelligent, well-educated and charismatic, with a biting sense of humor. He studied at Georgetown, Yale and Oxford Universities and holds a doctor-in-law degree from Oxford.

Berríos is extremely versatile and adapts well to all media and different audiences. He is author of a book, *Puerto Rican Independence: The Reason and the Struggle*, published in 1983, which traces the history of the independence movement in Puerto Rico. He has written many articles for the print media, from house organs to scholarly journals. He is equally effective in radio addresses and television interviews, and in various formats: debate, oratory, discussion, briefings or press conferences. He is equally at home with high school students or Harvard or Woodrow Wilson Center scholars, before sophisticated journalists or island *jíbaros,* defending a bill in the Puerto Rican Senate or testifying before the U.S. Congress.

Humor, hyperbole and ridicule give his presentations a sharp cutting edge, but he is equally capable of the serious political analysis of a legal brief. A good example of the latter is his 1973 speech before the American Society of International Law, in which he makes a strong case for his contention that Puerto Rico has not yet exercised its right of self-determination.[4]

Berríos sees independence as inevitable for Puerto Rico. He sums up his views as follows in an article in April 1977 *Foreign Affairs:*

"The dynamics of the Puerto Rican reality — economic disruption, social decay, the political disrepute of Commonwealth status, the impossibility of statehood as an alternative, the enormous cost of Commonwealth to the American tax-payer as a subsidy to a few corporations, the unacceptability of colonialism in the world community, and the merging of the independence ideal with the doctrine of democratic socialism — make of independence not only the inalienable right of the people of Puerto Rico, but also the only rational solution to the status problem of Puerto Rico."[5]

Berríos contends that two Reagan policies taken together — the Caribbean Basin Initiative and the New Federalism — effectively destroy the rationale for both the Free Associated State and statehood. By guaranteeing Caribbean countries free access to the U.S. market for many of their products, Reagan, he says, has undermined the "common market" rationale for free association. By placing more economic burdens on the states, the President, he contends, has sabotaged the statehood argument that being a state of the federal union would bring more economic benefits to Puerto Rico.[6]

Berríos' promotion of independence for Puerto Rico is coupled with strong criticism of the United States. He claims that U.S. policy toward Puerto Rico follows the dictates of U.S. corporations and the U.S. Navy. He accuses the United States of "militarizing" Puerto Rico, that is, preparing Puerto Rico as a base for projecting U.S. power into the Caribbean region. He was critical of the use of facilities in Puerto Rico for the invasion of Grenada, of sending the Puerto Rican National Guard to El Salvador on maneuvers, and of what he interprets as the preparation of young Puerto Ricans to fight against their Latin American "brethren" in Nicaragua.[7]

In 1985, Berríos in the Senate and Representative David Noriega, his counterpart in the House, introduced resolutions in their respective chambers for the withdrawal of U.S. forces from the island of Vieques and condemning the use of the U.S. Naval Station at Roosevelt Roads for military exercises on that island. The resolution called on President Reagan and the Department of Defense to terminate its target practice on Vieques, to transfer all federal land there to its inhabitants, and to indemnify them for damages suffered by the military presence on the island. The resolution did not prosper in either house and Berríos directed his criticism at Governor Hernández Colón for being a "lackey" of American imperialism for not having supported it.

When, in 1985, the *New York Times* broke the story of U.S.

contingency plans to deploy nuclear arms in Puerto Rico in the event of an emergency, Berríos, along with Popular Democratic Party Senator Gilberto Rivera Ortiz, prepared another resolution, this one asking President Reagan for his interpretation of the Treaty of Tlatelolco prohibiting the stationing of nuclear arms in Latin America, as it applies to Puerto Rico, and for the president's assurance that the Treaty was being scrupulously observed. This resolution passed the Senate. Rivera Ortiz was sent to Washington and was given the assurance requested.[9]

Another task to which Berríos has dedicated major effort has been what he terms the "internationalization," especially the "Latinamericanization," of the quest for Puerto Rican independence.

One of Berríos' many "hats" is that of Vice President of the Permanent Conference of Latin American Political Parties, better known by its Spanish acronym, COPPAL. At a meeting in La Paz, Bolivia, on October 12, 1982, COPPAL passed a unanimous resolution

1. reaffirming its unequivocal support for Puerto Rican independence;
2. repeating its demand that the UN General Assembly place the case of Puerto Rico's colonialism on its agenda;
3. instructing Rubén Berríos, as vice president of COPPAL, in name of and in representation of all political parties which make up the organization, to carry out all necessary negotiations before governments and international organizations to obtain effective support for Puerto Rican independence and discussion of the Puerto Rican case in the UN General Assembly.[10]

At that time COPPAL represented 29 Latin American political parties, most of which were social democratic and eight of which (those in Belize, Bolivia, Colombia, Grenada, México, Nicaragua, Panamá and the Dominican Republic) controlled the government.

The resolution authorized Berríos to travel throughout Latin America and the Caribbean seeking support for Puerto Rican independence, not only in the name of the Puerto Rican Independence Party, of which he is president, but also in the name of the millions of Latin Americans represented by the member parties of COPPAL.

Two months later, Berríos met with Colombian President Belisario Betancur and Cuban President Fidel Castro.[11] Berríos said that his interview with the Colombian president produced a promise to consider supporting a demand that the UN General Assembly review Puerto Rico's political status. While in Colombia, Berríos addressed a meeting of the Congress of Latin American Workers (CLAT) which subsequently passed a resolution in favor of independence for Puerto Rico. Berríos said his interview with Castro lasted three and a half hours, during which the Cuban president, who has made Puerto Rican independence one of his foremost policy objectives since taking power, reportedly reiterated his "unbreakable support" for Berríos' cause.[12]

Berríos said he would continue his campaign with visits to Venezuela, Panamá, México, Ecuador, Perú and the Dominican Republic. "Our purpose," he said, "is that all Latin American governments who respect the tradition of Bolivar, be they conservative, center or leftist, support Puerto Rican independence."[13]

In early 1983, Berríos attended the meeting of the foreign ministers of the Movement of Non-aligned Nations in Managua, Nicaragua, in his capacity of vice president of COPPAL. In an interview with United Press International he accused the United States of using Puerto Ricans as cannon fodder by requiring them to join the U.S. armed forces to participate in wars in which the United States finds itself.[14]

Berríos said the people of Puerto Rico expect the imminent regionalization of the war in Central America. This, he said, "will cause an enormous uprising among the people; it will be a milestone in our country's struggle against imperialism."[15]

"The United States," he said, "is in Puerto Rico for the geopolitical control of Latin America and to have a military base and have an overwhelming force in our country."[16]

He said that the people of Puerto Rico have their hands tied to their shoulders. "We have accomplished material things, but with our hands tied. We need to free ourselves and work for ourselves and not for U.S. multinationals. We can subsist as a republic, but we can not subsist without freeing ourselves."[17]

The United States, he said, is to blame for the 40% real unemployment in Puerto Rico. He said that U.S. companies take out each year more than half the profit made in Puerto Rico.[18]

The news agency EFE reported that a paragraph in support of

Puerto Rico would be included in the meeting's final resolution.[19]

The Puerto Rican Independence Party became a member of the Socialist International in 1983 after seven years of trying to gain acceptance. That same year it succeeded in persuading the Socialist Congress to pronounce itself in favor of Puerto Rico's "struggle for independence." At the biennial congress in Perú June 20-24, 1986, the PIP was able to get through a resolution in unanimous support of the August 1985 UN Decolonization Committee resolution reaffirming "the inalienable right of the people of Puerto Rico to self-determination and independence."[20]

Berríos has frequently testified before the UN Decolonization Committee and has worked with the Cuban and Venezuelan delegations to the United Nations on resolutions condemning the United States with respect to its policies and activities in Puerto Rico.

In 1985, Berríos announced a major change in PIP electoral strategy. At an assembly in Loiza, a small village near San Juan, he asserted that the Puerto Rican electorate has two main concerns: clean, efficient government and solution of the problem of political status. Without abandoning its independence objective, the party will adopt fulfillment of these goals as its strategy for the 1988 election, he said.

"We will use the elections as a means of electing an honest and decent government," he asserted, "with a mandate to convoke, within a fixed time period, a People's Assembly to be elected exclusively to solve the status problem."[21]

In short, Berríos pledged that the PIP will not promote independence as such in the 1988 campaign, just good government and a promise of a separate People's Assembly to deal with status. Thus, the PIP hopes to broaden its appeal to all who share these objectives, regardless of party.[22] For the 1986 PIP general assembly, which celebrated the 40th anniversary of the party's foundation, Berríos invited the Nicaraguan Minister of Culture, Ernesto Cardenal, to give the keynote address. Cardenal called upon the assembled to adopt the revolutionary slogan, "a free Puerto Rico, or death."

Berríos has already established common ground with the *independentista* wing of the Popular Democratic Party. In an interview over Ponce radio, Berríos indicated that he was ready to accept "the convenience of free association as a formula of transition toward independence."[23] A meeting of minds occurred when Severo Colberg, leader of the PDP left, said that he visualizes "culminated Commonwealth" as a step toward independence.[24]

Position of Fernando Martín García

Fernando Martín is vice president and secretary for international relations of the Puerto Rican Independence Party and was the party's candidate for governor in 1984, receiving about 4 percent of the vote for that office. Martín does not have the skills and charisma of Berríos, but there is no doubt that he is his loyal follower. His language toward the United States is as abusive,[25] and he is a firm supporter of Berríos' new electoral strategy.[26] He has substituted for Berríos at many events and accompanied him on his trip to Cuba in 1982, as well as on trips to the United Nations. The only discrepancy of note between the two men is in their outlook toward changes in the present Commonwealth status. While Berríos is willing to accept any change which would constitute a step toward independence, Martín considers that any plan to use the Compact of Free Association of Micronesia and the Marshall Islands as a precedent for Puerto Rico would be "highly dangerous."[27]

Position of David Noriega

Representative David Noriega is the third of the PIP triumvirate. He has co-sponsored legislation with Berríos and with sympathetic colleagues in the House, for example, resolutions to investigate the possibility of U.S. nuclear arms at Roosevelt Roads and a bill in opposition to the construction of Voice of America facilities at Cabo Rojo in southwestern Puerto Rico. Noriega called the proposed relay station "a radio of aggression against the peoples of Latin America." The resolution was forgotten when the nature of the Voice of America was better understood and VOA officials were able to quiet fears with respect to the construction and operation of the facility.

Position of the Puerto Rican Socialist Party (PSP)

As stated previously, the Puerto Rican Socialist Party is not a political party but rather a marxist political movement. It has worked closely with Communist Cuba at the United Nations and at Third World forums to condemn U.S. policy toward and activities in Puerto Rico. The PSP is not interested in a period of transition to independence. It insists on the immediate, total and unconditional transfer of all political power to the people of Puerto Rico and has refused to renounce violence as a weapon in the "revolutionary struggle" for independence. It is much more militant than the PIP and serves as the intellectual inspiration for Puerto Rican terrorist groups. Its following is miniscule since all but a very few in Puerto Rico reject either marxism or political violence or both. The "party" is composed mainly of attorneys, university students and so-called intellectuals.

The PSP has two principal leaders: Juan Mari Bras, its former Secretary General, and Carlos Gallisá, who currently occupies that office.

Juan Mari Bras, a prominent attorney who has led the radical wing of the Puerto Rican independence movement for many years, is now semi-retired from politics, though he still appears on many committees, television shows, public panels and seminars when the sponsors of such events feel that the marxist or radical viewpoint should be presented, or that all four "political parties" should be represented, or because of the personal attraction of Mari Bras as a colorful public figure still lucid in his exposition of *independentista* ideals. He is the author of two books, *El Otro Colonialismo* (1982) and *La Asamblea Constituyente* (1986). The first chronicles the PSP search for support at the United Nations and in the Non-aligned Movement. The second discusses the use of the constituent assembly as a vehicle for consensus in Puerto Rico in past years.

Mari Bras has stated that when the time comes, the PSP will organize a Socialist Workers Republic and declare its existence without any felt need to ask permission of any agency of the U.S. Government. The right to independence is well-established, he avers, and there is no need to enter into negotiations with anyone to achieve it.[29]

"We would proclaim independence," he has said, "then we would appoint two commissions. One would go to the United Nations to demand international recognition. The other would go to Washington to negotiate with the United States the terms for a future relationship between the Republic of Puerto Rico and the United States. We would not negotiate independence because we do not feel that it has to be negotiated.[30]

"I think Puerto Rican independence is inevitable. Historically

125

speaking, the crisis in the colonial system is irreversible. There is no way to solve it under the existing system and patterns. The alternatives for the people of Puerto Rico are independence or total collapse of Puerto Rico as a country.[31]

"'The Puerto Rican Independence Party now favors an easy, reformist transition into independence, which would leave intact the system and economic structure of a capitalist Puerto Rico. The PSP insists on a revolutionary change that will completely transform these structures. We believe in bringing together three aspects of a single ideology — independence, socialism and revolution.[32]

"The independence struggle has been frustrated in the past because it was not socialist, and socialism has been frustrated because it was not independence oriented. Both were frustrated because neither was revolutionary. Both things (independence and socialism) must go together, and must be brought about by a method in keeping with the importance of our objective. One can not aspire to anything as radical as independence and socialism except through revolution. Only revolutions have brought the great changes in history, and the situation in Puerto Rico requires a revolutionary change.'"[33]

At the time of the arrest of the *Macheteros* in Puerto Rico by the F.B.I. in 1985, Mari Bras reiterated his support for armed struggle for the independence of Puerto Rico, including the right to receive arms from Cuba. "In order to have a Republic by 1992," he said, "we will have to have an armed struggle. Without it, there is no use talking about a republic by that date."[34]

Mari Bras contends that statehood would never be recognized by the United Nations as a means to decolonize Puerto Rico.

"Statehood is not a formula for decolonization but rather the culmination of colonial domination. In the case of East Timor, the United Nations resolved that the integration of a colonial territory to the administrative power is not a valid alternative when the colonial domination was initiated through armed invasion. This is exactly what happened in Puerto Rico."[35]

Mari Bras believes that Governor Hernández Colón should make more use of his Caribbean economic development program to pressure political status concessions from Washington.

"This moment offers a magnificent opportunity to the Hernández Colón administration to launch an initiative for the conquest of broader powers for the Commonwealth... but he has to take a much

126

more audacious policy than he is now following...

"The concessions that Hernández Colón should now demand from the United States should be defined in a constituent assembly."[36]

In the view of Mari Bras, this assembly should take place in 1989. Local law makers would petition that Puerto Rico be granted the power to negotiate trade treaties and impose tariffs to protect island industry from an "invasion" of foreign competition. He said that *independentista* participation in such an assembly could be highly influential because neither of the other two tendencies — autonomy and statehood — enjoys majority control.[37] Such an assembly, he believes, would break the current stalemate over status and give the island more negotiating power with the United States by creating a body of delegates to whom the United States would have to explain its decisions.[38]

Carlos Gallisá, a young attorney who replaced Mari Bras as Secretary General of the Puerto Rican Socialist Party, is even more militant than his predecessor.

"The U.S. military-industrial complex," he states, "is the principal force insisting that Puerto Rico remain a colony, since investors obtain millions of dollars a year [from Puerto Rico] and have in Vieques and Ceiba [Roosevelt Roads] their largest base in the hemisphere...

"The U.S. Government," he says, "has the responsibility of starting the process of decolonization by withdrawing its occupation forces from Puerto Rico."[39]

Gallisá has accused the United States of trying to convert Puerto Rico into a military department. He cites as evidence the "announced" reactivation of Ramey Air Force Base, the possible transfer of the U.S. Army School of the Americas from Panamá to Puerto Rico, the renewed use of communications towers on the western shores of Puerto Rico, the announcement by former Governor Luis A. Ferré of the possible establishment in Puerto Rico of industries for the manufacture of military wearing apparel, and increased recruitment in public schools of young people for military service. All this, he has said, may lead to the future annexation of Puerto Rico as a northamerican "geopolitical and military necessity."[40]

Gallisá has called the agreement between the Government of

Puerto Rico and the U.S. Navy that limits shelling on the island of Vieques "a smokescreen to mislead the people of Puerto Rico and to make them believe that the abuses and outrages against the people there are over."[41]

With respect to U.S. contingency plans for introducing nuclear weapons into Puerto Rico in case of emergency, Gallisá has accused Governor Hernández Colón of being an accomplice of the United States in the violation of the Treaty of Tlatelolco which prohibits the stationing of such arms in Latin America.[42]

Gallisá has repudiated indiscriminate terrorism but has affirmed that "armed struggle is an instrument of exploited peoples," and that "this is a form of struggle that a people can decide to use."[43] He has supported the actions of the *Macheteros*, comparing them to George Washington and the Latin American heroes, José Marti, Simón Bolívar and San Martin. He has also said that there was a "political justification" for the assassination of U.S. marines at Sabana Seca, for which the *Macheteros* have taken "credit."[44] He called the bombing of two U.S. military installations on October 28, 1986 a legitimate reaction of the people of Puerto Rico to the possible training of *Contra* rebels in Puerto Rico and to federal plans to cut down trees for commercial lumbering in the Caribbean National Forest (El Yunque).[45]

"When Puerto Rico is free," Gallisá has said, "no one will call those who took these and other armed actions terrorists; rather, they will say they were patriots."[46]

When, in April 1986, police undercover agent González Malavé was killed, presumably by *independentistas*, the assassination was deplored by all principal political figures in Puerto Rico except Gallisá, who called the act an "execution."[47]

Gallisá was among those who testified at the 1986 hearings on Puerto Rico conducted by the Committee on Interior and Insular Affairs of the U.S. House of Representatives. The following excerpts from his testimony sum up his position:

"The definition of territory within the context of the Constitution and law of the United States can not obscure the real issue of the political situation of Puerto Rico as a colony of the United States.

"The United States is a colonial power as it maintains the Puerto Rican people under the sovereign powers of Congress. These congressional powers are exercised by an act of conquest — the invasion of Puerto Rico during the Spanish-American War in 1898...

"The U.S. Government uses double-talk with regard to the political situation in Puerto Rico. This committee and Congress examines the political status of Puerto Rico as an issue, and the General Accounting Office states that 'the ultimate political status' of the territories has not yet been determined. Meanwhile, the State Department tells the General Assembly of the United Nations and the Decolonization Committee of the United Nations that the status of Puerto Rico is not an issue, as the people of Puerto Rico have exercised their right of self-determination in 1952...

"...self-determination should comply with the principles and requirements adopted by the United Nations in its Charter and in the several resolutions and decisions concerning decolonization, specifically relating to Puerto Rico.

"That means that all powers and authority presumably exercised by the three branches of government of the United States, legislative, judicial and executive, and all of its agencies and instrumentalities, including the armed forces of the United States, over the territory of Puerto Rico should be relinquished and transferred unconditionally and without reservations to the people of Puerto Rico, in order to allow them to fully exercise their inalienable right to self-determination and independence, in accordance with their freely expressed will and desire...

"I want to emphasize that there can be no self-determination if there is no withdrawal of the U.S. intervention in the Puerto Rican affairs and the process is preceded by a total transfer of powers of the Federal Government to the people of Puerto Rico.   "

"If the U.S. Government wants a peaceful transition for the decolonization of Puerto Rico, it is the responsibility of Congress and The White House to take the initial and necessary steps and actions toward that end...

"If the U.S. Government insists in maintaining the colonial domain in Puerto Rico, our struggle for independence will continue. We will use all means to achieve the freedom of our country. It is our right. And the same right that the people of the thirteen colonies exercised to liberate themselves from the colonial rule of England.

"As of today, there are over thirty-five Puerto Rican patriots incarcerated in the United States. The repression of the Federal authorities in Puerto Rico and in the United States toward the pro-independence fighters is not going to put an end to our struggle for independence."[48]

Position of the Puerto Rican United Nations Committee

The Puerto Rican United Nations Committee coordinates the position of the various pro-independence groups dealing with the Puerto Rican question at the United Nations. Its president is José Milton Soltero. The organization's position is reflected in the following excerpts from a message sent by Soltero to the First Latin American Congress on Anti-imperialist Thought, which met in Managua in February, 1985:

"The Government of the United States has ignored petitions for justice for Puerto Rico made by the United Nations Special Committee on Decolonization. Not only has it failed to respond favorably to claims in various United Nations resolutions, but it also has intensified in an impetuous, annexionist offensive, multiple political, economic, military and cultural maneuvers designed to dislodge Puerto Rico from the Latin American sphere and establish it even more solidly as an insular ghetto of the United States.

"The policy of the United States has the objective of expanding the frontiers of this country to the eastern part of the Caribbean, with the eventual incorporation of Puerto Rico as a state [overseas province] of the United States...

"A great debate has arisen in Puerto Rico and the United States regarding information published in the newspaper, 'The New York Times,' of New York, in which a report of the United States Government is made public, which admits that the Pentagon has been using Puerto Rico as a contingency staging area to initiate nuclear attacks against prospective enemies of that country in any future war, declared or undeclared. Such use constitutes a flagrant violation of the Tlatelolco Treaty on the Denuclearization of Latin America...

"In addition to using Puerto Rico as a center for nuclear arms activity in violation of the reference treaty, Washington violated existing international law and norms adopted repeatedly by the United Nations in using Puerto Rico, which is a territory which has not achieved its independence and therefore a colonial territory, as a center for military activity of an aggressive nature.

"Months before, trials were held in Puerto Rico for the U.S.

invasion of Grenada. Our territory has been used to train troops and for maneuvers in preparation for invasion plans against Nicaragua, Central America in general, and the Caribbean area.

"Moreover, the so-called Puerto Rican National Guard, which is legally defined as the militia of the Free Associated State, and whose Commander-in-Chief is the Governor of Puerto Rico, has been mobilized, and some of its units have been transferred to Panamá and to unknown locations in Central America in missions completely foreign to that of protecting the territory of Puerto Rico...

"The strategy which the United States applies to Puerto Rico... consists fundamentally in continuing to procrastinate in its obligation to fulfill its mandate to decolonize, while accelerating steps directed toward separating Puerto Rico from the Caribbean and Latin America...

"Puerto Rican independence is indispensable to assuring the national sovereignty of all Latin American people. In this way, the people of Latin America start to understand fully the need to Latinamericanize Puerto Rico's claim to decolonization and national sovereignty.

"When we speak of Latinamericanizing the demand for decolonization and sovereignty for Puerto Rico, we want to stress that this has to convert itself into a common cause for all nations of our America, above all differences of ideology, the diversity of existing systems and the geographic location of all Latin American countries...

"The struggle for Puerto Rican independence is the fulcrum and vanguard of the anti-imperialist struggle on our continent and the Caribbean...

"The Puerto Rican United Nations Committee hereby requests the delegates meeting in this historic First Latin American Congress on Anti-imperialist Thought to transmit to their respective people, to social organizations which you represent, as well as to governments, the need to support the proposal for Puerto Rican decolonization and full sovereignty in the United Nations."

Position of the Puerto Rican Bar Association

The *Colegio de Abogados* of Puerto Rico is an association to which all attorneys in Puerto Rico must belong in order to practice their profession. It is financed principally through member dues and remission by the Government of Puerto Rico of fees charged the public by the Treasury of Puerto Rico for stamps on legal documents. Since most members of the Puerto Rican legislature are among the 7,000 attorneys who belong to the association, it is perhaps the most powerful pressure group in Puerto Rico.

The *Colegio* was set up in 1842 to promote the interests of the legal profession. But it has a long history of involvement in Puerto Rican politics. It has organized committees to investigate questions regarding the status of Puerto Rico. The association claims that these committees represent all points of view on the issue, and indeed, careful examination of the backgrounds of committee members usually reveals at least one person who can be identified with each of the status options. However, independence activists usually dominate such committees, especially the international committee which deals with U.S.-Puerto Rican relations. For this reason, the Puerto Rican Bar Association is discussed under the independence option.

In theory, the facilities of the Bar Association are available to any group seeking a meeting place, and it has become a preferred spot for holding press conferences. It is a fact, however, that most activities at the *Colegio,* or sponsored by the *Colegio*, have strong independence overtones. An example is the First Puerto Rican Conference on Decolonization, held August 7, 1981. Its goals were defined as "to stop annexation" (i.e.statehood). It produced an agreement between PSP and PPD "autonomists" on tactics for hearings before the United Nations Decolonization Committee in New York.[49] The president of the Bar Association testified before this committee in the name of all practicing attorneys in Puerto Rico. Likewise, in 1986, the president of the association testified before the U.S. House Interior and Insular Affairs Committee in the name of the organization in favor of sovereignty for Puerto Rico.

An attorney identified with the independence movement headed a two-year Bar Association study which concluded that U.S. military activities in Puerto Rico are "contrary in letter and spirit" to the Treaty of Tlatelolco.[50]

Pro-independence members of the Bar Association have met with the presidents of the Puerto Rican House and Senate, and with the Governor of Puerto Rico, to press for a constituent assembly to resolve Puerto Rico's status dilemma.[51] Senator Rubén Berríos and Representative David Noriega jointly introduced a resolution in

March 1987 to place convocation of such an assembly on the 1988 ballot for voter approval, but it is not believed that the measure will prosper since both Governor Hernández Colón and NPP leaders have expressed strong opposition.[52]

On May 24, 1987, on the occasion of the visit to Puerto Rico of the King and Queen of Spain, the advertisement that follows appeared in the *El Mundo* newspaper. It was signed by leaders of 21 pro-independence groups, and in a personal capacity by five prominent members of the Bar Association. The Bar Association signers were its president, its vice president, a former president and the chairmen of two of its principal committees: constitutional law and international relations.

Welcome to the Puerto Rican Nation

"The signatories below, representing cultural, intellectual and trade union groups of different political and ideological tendencies in Puerto Rico, welcome to our country a sister nation and other hispano-american nations.

"This is a people that wishes to sustain cultural and all types of relations with the peoples of America and the world, but many times it is impossible to do so because of decisions foreign to its own interests, taken by officials of the U.S. Government. Among other things, this government, from Washington, refuses to grant entry visas to Puerto Rican national territory to foreign intellectuals that have been invited by universities and cultural groups of the country. Neither does it authorize Puerto Rico to make commercial treaties with other sovereign countries.

"Ours is a nation which does not take initiatives of military, ideological, commercial or other type of aggression against sister nations. It was not the government nor the people of Puerto Rico which decided to undertake the war maneuvers, Solid Shield, the establishment of the radio station, Voice of America, in Cabo Rojo, in the southwest part of the island, or the sending of troops from our territory to attack other American nations. We protest the storage of nuclear arms in our nation that places in peril our lives, and that of others. We wish to live in peace with our neighbors.

"Puerto Rico is a nation which seeks self-determination within the context of the economic, political and social realities of the region. Therefore, this Latin American and Caribbean people ask in Spanish, your native language, for your support for keeping our island open to all currents of opinion, facilitating for us contacts and the international forums necessary to continue breaking the cultural isolation to which we have been submitted. We claim our right to decide our political destiny for ourselves.''

The current president of the Bar Association, Ponce attorney Héctor Lugo Bougal, is a strong believer in independence for Puerto Rico.[53]

Position of the United States

The United States asserts that Puerto Rico is not a colony, that it exercised its right of self-determination when it chose the present free association arrangement with the United States. This was recognized by the United Nations in 1953, when that body removed Puerto Rico from its list of non-self-governing territories. Thus, the United States considers any attempt by the United Nations to reopen the question of Puerto Rico's status to constitute interference by that organization in the internal affairs of the United States and Puerto Rico — a kind of action specifically prohibited by Article 2 of the United Nations Charter.

In any event, the United States maintains, Puerto Rican independence can be had for the asking, citing repeated statements by U.S. presidents and the U.S. Congress to that effect. The United States points to the Philippines as an example of a territory which requested and was granted its independence from the United States. Since no elected government of Puerto Rico has ever requested independence, and since public opinion polls and election results show that no more than five to ten percent of the people of Puerto Rico support independence, the United States refuses to force independence on Puerto Rico against the will of 90 to 95 percent of its population. Such a step, the United States avers, would fly in the face of the right of self-determination.

This position was firmly stated by U.S. Ambassador Harvey J. Feldman, Alternate U.S. Representative to the United Nations General Assembly, on December 4, 1984:

''My delegation deeply resents the efforts of those Cold War warriors who seek to interfere in the internal affairs of the Commonwealth of Puerto Rico, a completely self-governing territory, where repeated acts of self-determination have taken place and been recognized by this body, and where free and fair elections are held every four years. In these elections, the Puerto Rican people do not have to choose from a single slate of candidates, but instead from a multiplicity of ideological and political stands. We recognize no right to interfere in these internal affairs. In view of repeated action by this Assembly, we consider the attempts by some to have the Special Committee, or the Fourth Committee take up Puerto Rico to be completely *ultra vires*. So, too, would we regard any attempt to drag this matter in through the back door by having the Secretariat prepare a special report. Those who have adopted this tactic should be aware that it is no more legitimate than would be an instruction to the Secretariat to prepare a special report on the separation of Slovakia or independence for Kazakhstan."[54]

In 1985, U.S. Ambassador to the United Nations Vernon Walters sent a letter to Abdul Koroma of Sierra Leone, President of the UN Decolonization Committee, protesting the reopening of debate on the Puerto Rican question.[55]

"One needs an extraordinary imagination," he said, "to consider Puerto Rico a colony. The resolution to that effect was rejected the last time in the General Assembly, and if Cuba presents it again, I think it will be rejected again."

Walters stated that Puerto Rico had held several elections confirming its present status of free association with the United States. He said that Puerto Rican nationalists had received barely one percent of the vote in the last election of 1984.

In the U.S. Congress, the foremost proponent of independence for Puerto Rico is Representative Ronald Dellums, Democrat of California. As previously mentioned, he has introduced a resolution calling for Puerto Rican independence into every session of the U.S. Congress for the past ten years. He has also testified in favor of independence for Puerto Rico before the UN Decolonization Committee. Dellums' 1985 resolution before Congress called for a plebiscite on the island to allow Puerto Rico to express its self-determination on what its future political status should be.

One potential candidate for U.S. President in 1988, the Reverend Jesse Jackson, has expressed himself in strong terms in favor of Puerto Rican independence. In August 1985, Jackson spent three days in Puerto Rico as guest of the Puerto Rican Bar Association. He called for the immediate transfer of all federal power to the government of Puerto Rico and denounced U.S. Navy maneuvers on Vieques and "perverted [U.S.] policies in Central America and the Caribbean," deeming them terrorist in nature.[56] In August 1986, Jackson testified before the UN Decolonization Committee and compared the situation in Puerto Rico with that of the blacks in South Africa.[57]

There is a precedent for the United States granting independence to one of its overseas territories, namely the Philippines, in 1946. A quick review of the conditions under which Congress granted independence to the Philippines is instructive as to past U.S. attitudes toward the independence option.

Revolutionary forces under the command of Emilio Aguinaldo wrested control of the Philippine archipelago from Spain during the period between the U.S. victory over the Spanish fleet in Manila Harbor May 1, 1898 and the signing of the Treaty of Paris on December 10, 1898, by which Spain ceded the islands to the United States and placed them under the administration of the U.S. Congress. The Filipinos clearly expected the United States to recognize their sovereignty. The United States did not know what to do. Finally, because of the underdevelopment of the islands, and because both Great Britain and Germany were eyeing them with envy, the United States decided to take control until conditions for independence were more auspicious. The result was a long and bloody war in which both sides committed numerous atrocities. The bitterness engendered by the conflict has soured U.S.-Filipino relations to this day.[58]

On March 24, 1934, a blueprint for Philippine independence was created by a Philippine Independence Act. A 10-year transitional period was established and the Philippine legislature was authorized to draft a Commonwealth-type of constitution. Steps were taken to cushion the effect of the loss of U.S. trade by the Philippines, and an immigration quota of 20,000 per year was set for the Philippines in 1965.

The Philippines actually achieved independence on July 4, 1946, but the land had been devastated during the Second World War. Congress assisted with a Rehabilitation Act providing up to $100 million worth of property, compensation totalling $400 million, and

$120 million for restoring public property and essential services. A new trade act continued duty-free exchange between the United States and the Philippines for eight years, to be phased out in 1974, thus extending the total transition period to 28 years.

United States citizens were entitled to the same privileges as Filipinos in developing public lands and natural resources and in operating public utilities. The exchange rate could not be altered except by Presidential concurrence. The United States acquired military bases on the islands. As a concession to the Philippine economy, the United States in 1955 slowed down the application of U.S. tariff rates on Philippine exports, while accelerating the time period for full application of Philippine duties on U.S. products.

In summary, after a shaky start, Congress proved to be as generous in granting independence to the Philippines as it had been in granting statehood to the 37 states admitted to the federal union after the original 13.[59]

Prospects for Independence

Despite the psychological attraction of independence, its theoretical validity as a decolonization option and U.S. generosity in granting independence to the Philippines, independence has little or no attraction for the vast majority of the people of Puerto Rico. The island's inhabitants are not willing to sacrifice their U.S. citizenship and social and economic benefits for the unknown of independence. They have heard of miserable conditions in the neighboring Dominican Republic, which has been independent for over a hundred years, and in Haiti, independent for over a hundred and fifty years. They are not convinced that independence leads to greater prosperity.

Unfortunately for the independence option, independence, which in theory, at least, is a dignified means of self-determination, is associated in Puerto Rico with socialism, Communism and anti-Americanism. A small, truly nationalistic independence party advocating close ties with the United States, the Puerto Rican Union Party (PUP), formed by University of Puerto Rico professor Antonio J. González in the 1960's, received even fewer votes than the other *independentista* parties. Most Puerto Ricans are pro-American and frightened of marxism and Communism. They do not want to go the way of Cuba and Nicaragua.

The only way that independence could come to Puerto Rico would be through gradual, incremental political maneuvering by "autonomist" forces under the guise of obtaining greater political power for Puerto Rico. The proposal of a constituent assembly advanced by independence leaders is an example of such maneuvering. As Mari Bras has intimated, such an assembly could place independence advocates in the enviable position of holding the balance of power between statehood and free association delegates. However, if a plebiscite were held, either statehood or free association would triumph and proponents of independence would have no say in the status change.

Two specific demands by independence leaders are unlikely to be met, at least not in the way they have been presented. The first is a request for "indemnification" to Puerto Rico by the United States for past "exploitation." The second is insistence on a full transfer of political power to Puerto Rico before any plebiscite is held.

The United States might agree to generous transitional aid over an extended period, as it did with the Philippines. But it is difficult to imagine the United States capitulating to a demand for compensation for "past wrongs." U.S. treatment of Puerto Rico over the years, especially since World War II, has been very generous. If there has been any "exploitation," it has been on the part of the colony exploiting the metropolitan power, rather than the other way around.

The other *independentista* demand, that for a complete transfer of power to Puerto Rico before any plebiscite, is also unlikely to be met by the United States except as a terminal act. If the phrase is taken literally, complete transfer of power would imply total withdrawal of all official U.S. activity from the island. There would be no more federal benefits, no more postal service, no more traffic control at the airport, no more federal support of any kind. Economic life would come to a standstill. Is this the kind of atmosphere that the *independentistas* want before a status plebiscite? They have never been specific.

Critics of the idea of a full transfer of power from the United States to Puerto Rico call it "pre-independence." It would appear to be more than that. It would appear to be independence, itself. There is high probability that the United States would interpret such a request, if officially made, in this manner.

The United States would probably be prepared to allow international observers to monitor a status plebiscite from the standpoint of fairness, honesty and secrecy and non-interference by U.S. agencies in the electoral process. But insistence on anything more is likely to be seen by the U.S. Congress and The White House as reflecting a lack of trust and confidence in the national government. The Congress would probably let it be known that it would consider the complete transfer of all political power to Puerto Rico as constituting the disposition of the territory under Article IV, Section 3, paragraph (2) of the U.S. Constitution, and would probably feel little or no obligation to act favorably on any subsequent request for statehood or modified free association.

NOTES

Chapter IV

1. The best source of information on the basic position of the Puerto Rico Independence Party with respect to the status of Puerto Rico is the party's 1984 campaign platform, available from the party's headquarters in Puerto Nuevo, San Juan, P.R.

2. p. 1, *El Mundo,* January 3, 1985.

3. Palabras de Apertura al Pueblo, speech by Rubén Berríos at Loiza, Puerto Rico, November 10, 1985.

4. pp. 23 and 65, *The San Juan Star*, April 17, 1973.

5. p. 583, *Foreign Affairs*, April 1977, article, "Independence for Puerto Rico: the Only Solution."

6. p. 3, *The San Juan Star*, February 26, 1982.

7. p. 3-A, *El Mundo*, May 11, 1983 and p. 12AA, *El Mundo*, May 12, 1983.

8. p. 20, *El Nuevo Día*, March 14, 1983 and p. 9, *The San Juan Star*, April 17, 1985.

9. p. 3, *El Nuevo Día*, February 14, 1985 and p. 14, *El Mundo*, March 1, 1985.

10. p. 9-A, *El Mundo*, October 23, 1982.

11. p. 1, *El Mundo*, and p. 6, *The San Juan Star*, December 30, 1982.

12. p. 12-A, *El Mundo*, December 24, 1982.

13. p. 1, *El Mundo*, December 30, 1982.

14. p. 4-A, *El Mundo*, January 12, 1983.

15. *Ibid*.

16. *Ibid*.

17. *Ibid*.

18. *Ibid*.

19. p. 4-A, *El Mundo*, January 14, 1986.

20. p. 26, *The San Juan Star*, January 26, 1986.

21. p. 3, *The San Juan Star*, and p. 2, *El Mundo*, November 11, 1985. The full text of Berríos' speech, "Palabras de Apertura al Pueblo," is available in pamphlet form from the headquarters of the Puerto Rican Independence Party in Puerto Nuevo, San Juan, Puerto Rico.

22. For further information on this strategy, see p. 4, *El Nuevo Día*, November 24, 1985 and May 5, 1985, and p. 71, *El Nuevo Día*, May 15, 1986; p. 16, *The San Juan Star*, May 21, 1986; and p. 9, *El Mundo*, July 16, 1986.

23. p. 15, *El Mundo*, October 22, 1985.

24. *Ibid*.

25. p. 7-A, *El Mundo*, March 28, 1984, and p. 26, *El Nuevo Día*, April 25, 1984.

26. p. 45, *El Nuevo Día*, November 18, 1985.

27. p. 9, *El Mundo*, and p. 4, *El Nuevo Día*, July 8, 1985.

28. p. 36, *The San Juan Star*, July 18, 1985, and p. 8, *El Nuevo Día*, August 14, 1985.

29. p. 1-A, *El Mundo*, August 29, 1974.

30. p. 5, *The San Juan Star*, August 8, 1976.

31. *Ibid*.

32. *Ibid*.

33. *Ibid*.

34. p. 2, *El Nuevo Día*, September 6, 1985.

35. p. 10-A, *El Mundo*, September 3, 1981. Mari Bras overlooks the removal of Hawaii, a territory acquired by the United States through military pressure, from the UN General Assembly list of non-self governing territories, when Hawaii achieved statehood.

36. *The San Juan Star*, November 3, 1985.

37. *Ibid.*

38. p. 5, *The San Juan Star*, July 20, 1986.

39. p. 14, *El Nuevo Día*, May 30, 1981.

40. p. 3-A, *El Mundo*, May 7, 1983.

41. p. 9-A, *El Mundo*, and p. 25, *The San Juan Star*, October 13, 1983.

42. p. 5, *El Nuevo Día*, and p. 25, *El Mundo*, February 15, 1985.

43. p. 3-A, *El Mundo*, November 21, 1985.

44. p. 6, *El Nuevo Día*, September 8, 1986.

45. p. 2, *The San Juan Star*, October 30, 1986.

46. p. 6, *El Nuevo Día*, September 6, 1986.

47. p. 4, *El Mundo*, May 1, 1986.

48. Statement by Carlos Gallisá, Secretary General, Puerto Rican Socialist Party, to the U.S. Committee on Interior and Insular Affairs, April 10 1986.

49. p. 17, *The San Juan Star*, August 13, 1981.

50. p. 3, *The San Juan Star*, and p. 23, *El Nuevo Día*, August 29, 1984.

51. p. 10, *The San Juan Star*, August 2, 1986.

52. The text of the resolution appears on page 7, *El Mundo*, March 16, 1987.

53. p. 3, *The San Juan Star*, September 14, 1986.

54. Statement by Ambassador Harvey J. Feldman, Alternate U.S. Representative to the 39th Session of the United Nations General Assembly, in Plenary, on Item 18, "Declaration on the Granting of Independence to Colonial Countries and Peoples," December 4, 1984. Press release 157-(84) December 4, 1984, U.S. Mission to the United Nations.

55. p. 16, *El Nuevo Día*, August 16, 1985, and *El Mundo*, August 13, 1985.

56. p. 25, *The San Juan Star*, August 27, 1985.

57. p. 32, *The San Juan Star*, August 28, 1986.

58. p. 1-3, Gregor, James A. *Crisis in the Philippines*, Ethics and Public Policy Center, Washington, D.C., 1984.

59. pp. 46-54, *Experience of Past Territories can Assist Puerto Rico Status Deliberations*, Report to the Congress of the United States, Comptroller General, Washington, D.C., 1980.

141

Chapter V

AN ESCAPE FROM
THE COLONIAL DILEMMA

Every U.S. President since Dwight D. Eisenhower has pledged to respect the freely expressed will of the people of Puerto Rico with regard to their political future.

This is a well-known fact, and it impresses people. It appears to reflect the quintessence of democratic adherence to the sacred principle of self-determination of peoples, as conceived by Woodrow Wilson in his famous Fourteen Points and enshrined in international law in the charters of both the League of Nations and the United Nations.

For more than three decades, this statement has served as an argument-stopper for rebutting the accusation that the United States pursues a policy of colonialism with respect to Puerto Rico. Seven U.S. Presidents, and the U.S. Congress in a 1979 joint resolution, have promised to make a change in the political status of Puerto Rico if a request for change is ever made.

Could one ask for anything more?

The answer is a resounding yes, much more. This posture by the United States overlooks some basic inequities in the U.S.-Puerto Rican equation. In fact, the U.S. position of "Let them decide and we'll respond," is both escapist and irresponsible. At least four major adjustments in U.S. policy will be required if Puerto Rico is to escape from its status dilemma:

1. *The United States must realize that it is the United States and not Puerto Rico which bears the major responsibility, both moral and legal, for instituting changes in the U.S.-Puerto Rican relationship.*

In 1898 the U.S. Congress declared the war that brought the United States to the shores of Puerto Rico. In that same year, Congress accepted responsibility for Puerto Rico in the Treaty of Paris by which Spain ceded the island to the new conquerors. In 1917, the U.S. Congress granted U.S. citizenship to the island's inhabitants. In 1950, the U.S. Congress passed the two basic laws which establish the present relationship. These were U.S. actions, and the United States can not escape the responsibility for such actions. If there is discontent in Puerto Rico and the people of Puerto Rico are unable to agree on the steps to resolve their status problem, the United States has the moral and legal responsibility to try to help.

Such is the situation today in Puerto Rico. Because Puerto Rican political parties are under such tight rules of discipline, it would be necessary for one party to gain control of both the governorship and the two chambers of the legislature in order to effect a basic change in U.S.-Puerto Rican relations, or even to pass a new plebiscite law. If the party supporting the present status option happens to control these three "strong points," as was the case in the quadrennium beginning in 1984, no action is possible, even in the face of widespread dissatisfaction, if that party refuses to discuss the issue.

As a minimum, the United States should request Puerto Rico to hold a new status plebiscite, if only to fulfill its responsibility of keeping informed on the nature of status sentiment among the inhabitants, who are citizens of the United States and to whom the U.S. Congress owes a special obligation.

2. *The United States must recognize the inherent danger in letting the present situation drift.*

Though it may appear to be an illogical contradiction, in 1984 the American citizens in Puerto Rico elected a government which turned out to be anti-American, at least in terms of rejecting closer association with fellow-citizens on the mainland. This was not the intention of the voters. It was, rather, a consequence of the election. The vast majority of the people of Puerto Rico are friendly toward the United States, but the present government has fallen under the influence of the "autonomists" and *independentistas* within the left wing of the party in power. These elements want more political power for Puerto Rico, not within the framework of the U.S. political system but outside. Their demands run the gamut from cosmetic changes in the present free association arrangement all the way along the free association spectrum to an "associated republic" leading to independence. Unfortunately for both the United States and Puerto Rico, and for the independence movement itself, the quest for independence in Puerto Rico has strong anti-American overtones.

At the moment, the people of Puerto Rico are split between those friendly to the United States who seek more rights and powers within the U.S. political system and those who seek more rights and powers outside that framework. Such activity is particularly pronounced in the field of international relations. If the United States takes no action, Puerto Rico could evolve, incrementally and almost imperceptibly, into an independent, socialist anti-American regime. If this should happen, it is improbable that the United States could maintain its economic interests and military bases on the island. In time of crisis in the Caribbean, Puerto Rico's uncertain political status could serve as a pretext for invasion by a hostile power.

In fear of such developments, many middle class professional people are leaving Puerto Rico to resettle in the United States. Sometimes their motivation is the search for economic opportunity or a better quality of life. But fear of the associated republic, independence and marxism is another component of such decisions to leave. Some put it this way: "If statehood isn't coming to Puerto Rico, I'm going to statehood." The situation is comparable to Cuba just before and after Fidel Castro came to power. If the movement of the Puerto Rican government toward independence and socialism intensifies, so will the exodus of the Puerto Rican middle class. If it appears that a marxist regime will come to power, the migration of Puerto Ricans to the United States will dwarf the Mariel boatlift and any other previous immigration in U.S. history. And there will be no way to stop their entry, for these people will be fellow-U.S. citizens, fully entitled to enter the United States.

3. *The United States must realize that promises to respect the right of self-determination of the people of Puerto Rico, though essential, are not enough.*

Promises to act in accordance with the will of the people of Puerto Rico carries an obligation to keep oneself continuously informed as to the preferences of the people involved, so that policy can be elaborated in terms of the known will of the people at any given time. This implies a continuing process of inputs and outputs.

The U.S. Government accepts the results of a plebiscite held 20 years ago as though they were still valid today. During this period, a new generation of voters has been added to the electoral lists. Half of the people eligible to vote today did not vote in the 1967 plebiscite. They were too young. Some were not even born. Puerto Rico urgently needs another plebiscite. Sentiment on such a basic and burning issue should be measured at regular intervals.

Because of the fact that each of Puerto Rico's three principal parties advocates a particular status option, it is a common error to interpret a particular party's victory at the polls as popular endorsement of that party's status preference. This is not necessarily the case. Many different issues are involved in general elections in Puerto Rico, as elsewhere. Also, from time to time, one party or another will state flatly that "status is not an issue." For example, though victory by the pro-Commonwealth Popular Democratic Party in the 1984 elections has been widely interpreted on the U.S. mainland as reaffirmation of the *Estado Libre Asociado* by the people of Puerto Rico, two pro-statehood parties together received a greater number of votes. Furthermore, the Popular Democratic Party had pledged that if elected it would do nothing to change the status of Puerto Rico during its term of office. Thus, the party attracted many votes from those who favored independence but knew that the independence candidate for Governor could not win and cast their vote for the *Populares* in order to stop statehood at all costs. Such persons are called *melones* in Puerto Rico from their green exteriores and red interiores. Green and red are the colors, respectively, of the Puerto Rican Independence Party and the Popular Democratic Party.

The United States has said it will respect the right of the

people of Puerto Rico to self-determination, but what does this really mean?

President Carter has said that self-determination for Puerto Rico means "whatever decision the people of Puerto Rico may wish to take — statehood, independence, commonwealth status, or mutually-agreed modifications of that status — it will be yours, in accordance with your own tradition, democratically and peacefully."[1]

The statement is ambiguous and appears to contradict itself with respect to modifications in commonwealth status. How can a decision with respect to the modification of commonwealth status be "yours," in other words, Puerto Rico's, if such modifications must be "mutually-agreed" upon?

Carter seems to be saying that the United States will accept the unilateral will of Puerto Rico with respect to a shift of status to independence or statehood, or a continuation of the present commonwealth status as is, but that the United States reserves the right to veto any change within the free association spectrum. This indeed was the case with HB 11200 of the 94th Congress.

Likewise, in his January 12, 1982 Declaration to the people of Puerto Rico, President Reagan, while expressing a personal preference for statehood, stated that "this Administration will accept whatever choice is made by a majority of the island's population." Is this a blank check? Would the Reagan Administration, contrary to President Carter, automatically approve any modification of the current commonwealth status? An associated republic? A confederation between the United States and Puerto Rico on the model of the United Arab Republic of the 1950's?

4. *Both the United States and Puerto Rico must face the fact that the present commonwealth status is indefensible and untenable.*

One attitude encountered both in the United States and Puerto Rico is, "if it works, don't fix it." The problem is that Commonwealth, as it now exists, is not working and needs fixing. Puerto Rican political leaders may disagree about many things, but on one point there is almost universal agreement: the present version of free association is not serving the people of Puerto Rico well and should be modified.

In 1985, U.S. Ambassador to the United Nations, Vernon

147

Walters, was quoted as saying, "It would require extraordinary imagination to consider Puerto Rico a colony."[2]

The fact is: it would require extraordinary imagination to consider that Puerto Rico is not a colony.

Although there are many definitions of the concept, "colony," they all boil down to "a people under control of another people." The control can be partial or complete, but it always includes the critical areas of internal security, defense and foreign affairs. The colony may be exploited by the metropolitan power, or the metropolitan power may be extremely generous to the colony. This is immaterial. The determining factor is the existence of a *de jure* or *de facto* superior-inferior relationship which places the people of a given territory in a subordinate position to the people of another power. The essence is lack of equality in the relationship.

Most persons would accept the definition of "colony" listed in the authoritative and highly respected *International Relations Dictionary* authored by political scientists Jack C. Plano and Roy Olton of Western Michigan University: "a non-contiguous territorial possession of a sovereign state."[3]

There can be no question that Puerto Rico is a non-contiguous territorial possession of the United States. The island is separated from the U.S. mainland by over a thousand miles of ocean. Puerto Rico is a territory of the United States under both international and U.S. constitutional law. The political entity known as Puerto Rico is referred to as a territory in United Nations terminology. And the U.S. Constitution recognizes only two types of political units under its jurisdiction: states and territories. Since Puerto Rico is not a state, it must be a territory. Indeed, the U.S. Supreme Court has deemed Puerto Rico to be an un-incorporated territory of the United States,[4] and has ruled that U.S. citizens in Puerto can be treated differently from U.S. citizens living within a state.[5]

Puerto Rico became a possession of the United States in 1898 when the island was ceded to the United States by Spain. This status was reaffirmed in the Federal Relations Act of 1950 which, in its first Article, refers to Puerto Rico as "belonging to the United States..." The Treaty of Paris placed Puerto Rico under the control of the U.S. Congress, and the U.S. Constitution provides that "The Congress shall have the power to dispose of and make needful rules and regulations respecting the territory or other property belonging to the United States."[6]

The United States cites UN General Assembly Resolution 748 of 1953[7] as proof that Puerto Rico is not a colony. As a result of this resolution, Puerto Rico was removed from the Assembly's list of non-self-governing territories on which administering powers were required to report. But this resolution bears close reexamination, especially in terms of the evolution of international thought with respect to colonialism during the three decades since the resolution was passed.

UNGA Resolution 748 made a number of pleasant observations on the newly-created Free Associated State of Puerto Rico. It stated that Puerto Rico had reached a new constitutional status. It asserted that Puerto Rico had exercised its right of self-determination. It observed that Puerto Rico had been invested with "attributes of political sovereignty" which clearly identified its status as self-governing and an "autonomous political entity." On this basis, the Assembly removed Puerto Rico from its list of non-self-governing territories.

There is no question that Puerto Rico had reached a new constitutional status in 1953, since the island had adopted a new constitution in 1952. There is no question that this new Constitution, as well as U.S. Public Law 600 which authorized its establishment, had been approved by the people. Public Law 600 was approved in a referendum in 1951 and the Constitution in two referenda held in 1952.[8]

But there is serious question as to whether Puerto Rico had achieved a new, self-governing political status vis-a-vis the United States. U.S.-Puerto Rican relations are in fact still governed by the Jones Act of 1917, as amended. The pertinent provisions have been retitled "Federal Relations Act" but little or no change has been made in their content.

Legitimate questions also arise as to whether Puerto Rico's status as a Free Associated State conforms to the criteria for free association established by a companion resolution approved the very same day, UNGA Resolution 742 of November 27, 1953.

Part Three of the Annex of Resolution 742 states that the people of a non-autonomous territory who have associated themselves with a metropolitan power should have the freedom to modify their status. This has not been the case for Puerto Rico. Two requests for modification of the present status, the Fernos-Murray Bill of 1959 and the Pact for Permanent Union (HB 11200) of the 1970's were not acted upon by the U.S. Congress.

Part Three also states that a free association arrangement should be made by treaty or bilateral agreement. The Free Associate State of Puerto Rico was established by U.S. law.

Part Three calls for the extension of constitutional guarantees to the associated territory on an equal basis. This is not the case in the' non-incorporated territory of Puerto Rico.

Part Three calls for equal participation by the associated territory in any modification of the State's constitutional system. Puerto Rico has no input with respect to the amendment process to the U.S. Constitution.

Part Three calls for equal representation in central legislative organs. Puerto Rico has a Resident Commissioner without the right to vote in the U.S. Congress but is denied the two Senators and seven Representatives to which it is entitled under any formula for equal representation.

Part Three calls for equal rights of citizenship in the associated territory. U.S. citizens in Puerto Rico do not enjoy equal rights with U.S. citizens in the 50 states.

Part Three states that public officials of the territory should be admitted to public positions in the central authority. Puerto Ricans are not eligible for election to the positions of U.S. Representative and U.S. Senator.

Nevertheless, Resolution 748 was approved by a vote of 26 to 16 with 18 abstentions.[9] A total of 34 countries could not bring themselves to vote in favor of the measure.

Special note should be taken of the last paragraph of Resolution 748: The General Assembly "expresses its assurance that, in accordance with the spirit of the present resolution, the ideals embodied in the Charter of the United Nations, the traditions of the people of the United States of America and the political advancement attained by the people of Puerto Rico, due regard will be paid to the will of both the Puerto Rican and American peoples in the conduct of their relations under the present legal status, and also in the eventuality that either of the parties to the mutually agreed association may desire any change in the terms of this association."

The question arises as to whether the United States paid "due regard" to the will of the people of Puerto Rico when it failed to take action in 1976 on HB 11200, the Pact for Permanent Union between the United States and Puerto Rico, submitted by the Resident Commissioner of Puerto Rico to the U.S. Congress on behalf of the people of Puerto Rico.

Besides failing to meet all criteria of UNGA Resolutions 742 and 748 of 1953, the present free association agreement between the United States and Puerto Rico also fails to meet at least one of the criteria for free association set forth in UNGA Resolution 1541 of 1960.

The second paragraph of Principle VII of the Annex of this resolution reads:

"The associated territory should have the right to determine its internal constitution without outside interference, in accordance with due processes and the freely expressed wishes of the people."

This is not the case at present in Puerto Rico. Article VII, Section 3 of the Constitution of the Commonwealth of Puerto Rico reads in part:

"Any amendment or revision of this Constitution shall be consistent with the resolution enacted by the Congress of the United States approving this constitution, with the applicable provisions of the Constitution of the United States, with the Puerto Rican Federal Relations Act and with Public Law 600, Eighty-first Congress, adopted in the nature of a compact."

The only formal amendment made to the Constitution of Puerto Rico (that of lowering the voting age to 18 in 1969) presented no problem. But it is clear from the language of the constitution of the Commonwealth of Puerto Rico, as cited above, that Puerto Rico does not have the right to determine its internal constitution without outside interference.

There is no question that the present relationship between the United States and Puerto Rico is not one of equals and should be rectified. If the term "colony" is difficult to swallow, one can look at the situation in the positive sense of perfecting the relationship. In no way should the large amount of federal aid which

Puerto Rico receives from the United States obscure the fact that Puerto Rico is in an inferior political relationship to the United States. The situation is not only unjust and undignified; it is untenable by today's standards of human rights and acceptable conduct between peoples.

The present U.S. position is to remain neutral in Puerto Rico's status battle, but failure to insist on a new measurement of sentiment on the status issue (i.e. another plebiscite) has the effect of favoring the status quo, the present free association agreement. Asking Puerto Rico to hold a plebiscite would not constitute interference in Puerto Rico's internal affairs. Congress is responsible for the territories, and up-to-date and reliable information on the status preferences of the inhabitants of a territory is essential to the fulfillment of Congress' oversight responsibilities.

Congress must ask itself if it would ever accept any modification of the present free association agreement which would place it in conformity with Resolution 742 of 1953 and Resolution 1541 of 1960. The lukewarm reception which the Fernos-Murray Bill of 1959 and HB 11200 (the Pact for Permanent Union) of 1976 received in the U.S. Congress; the low esteem in which the United Nations is currently held in the United States; plus the difficulties of accommodating more autonomy for Puerto Rico, short of independence, within the present U.S. constitutional structure, would lead one to believe that there is no more interest in Congress today to modify free association arrangements with Puerto Rico than there has been in the past, and perhaps less.

If this analysis is correct, the time has come for the U.S. Congress to ask the people of Puerto Rico to choose between the two classic status options, statehood and independence, which present no problem in terms of international acceptance. Congress should indicate its readiness to accept Puerto Rico as the 51st State of the federal union, with generous transition provisions, but should also assure Puerto Rico that it would also accept the choice of independence, if that should be the will of the majority of the people on the island.

The most appropriate vehicle for expressing such sentiments may be a joint resolution of the U.S. Congress. It might read as follows:

JOINT RESOLUTION

Authorizing a Status Plebiscite in Puerto Rico

Whereas the Commonwealth relationship between the United States and Puerto Rico has served our people well for more than three decades;

Whereas there exists in Puerto Rico a strong desire to culminate this relationship in a manner that will permit the people of Puerto Rico, like people in the United States, to enjoy the fullest measure of social, economic and political rights and progress;

Whereas the nature of the present relationship has not always been understood by other nations in the world;

Whereas the Commonwealth relationship was originally conceived as a temporary arrangement pending a final decision on the future status of Puerto Rico;

Whereas any change in the present relationship should be made by mutual consent of the parties involved:

Therefore, be it resolved by the Senate and House of Representatives of the United States of America in Congress assembled

That a plebiscite be held in Puerto Rico as soon as possible and no later than 1989 between the status options of full statehood within the U.S. federal union, and full independence and sovereignty as a new nation state; and be it further resolved

That the United States would be pleased to welcome Puerto Rico as a new State of the United States but would fully respect the wishes and desires of the people of Puerto Rico if their choice is sovereign independence. End of Resolution.

The United States and Puerto Rico have been cohabitating for nearly a century. Now is the time to get married, or to separate.

NOTES

Chapter V

1. Message of President Jimmy Carter to the people of Puerto Rico on the occasion of the celebration of Constitution Day, July 25, 1978.

2. p. 12, *The San Juan Star*, August 18, 1985.

3. p. 26, *International Relations Dictionary* (third edition) by Jack C. Plano and Roy Olston, ABC-Clio, Inc., Santa Barbara, California, 1982.

4. Balzac v. People of Puerto Rico (258, U.S. 298), 1922.

5. Various Supreme Court decisions. The first in a long series were De Lima v. Bidell 182 U.S. 1 (1901); Downes v. Bidwell 182 U.S. 244 (1901); and Armstrong v. U.S. 182 U.S. 243 (1901). For a full discussion of rights and requirements of the U.S. Constitution which do or may apply to Puerto Rico in whole or in part, see *Report of the United States-Puerto Rico Commission on the Status of Puerto Rico, Government Printing Office*, Washington, D.C., August 1966, p. 45.

6. Article II, Section 3, paragraph (2), U.S. Constitution.

7. 459th Plenary Meeting, November 27, 1953.

8. pp. 118, 119 and 124, *The Status of Puerto Rico: Selected Background Studies*, U.S. Government Printing Office, Washington, D.C. 1966.

9. p. 27, *El Imparcial*, November 29, 1953.

Select Bibliography

Berríos, Rubén. *La Independencia de Puerto Rico: Razón y Lucha*. Editorial Línea, México, D.F., 1983.

Bothwell, Reece (ed.) *Puerto Rico: Cien Años de Lucha Política*. Editorial Universitaria, Universidad de Puerto Rico, Río Piedras, Puerto Rico, 1979.

Cabranes, José. "Out of the Colonial Closet," article in *Foreign Policy,* Number 33, Winter 1978-1979.

Carr, Raymond. *Puerto Rico: A Colonial Experiment*. New York University Press/Vintage Books, Random House, New York, 1984.

Clark, Truman. *Puerto Rico and the United States: 1917-1933*. University of Pittsburgh Press, Pittsburgh, Pa., 1975.

Comptroller General. *Report to the Congress of the United States: Experience of Past Territories Can Assist Puerto Rico Status Deliberations*. U.S. General Accounting Office, Washington, D.C., March 7, 1980.

_____ . *Report to the Congress of the United States: Puerto Rico's Political Future - A Divisive Issue with Many Dimensions*. GGD-81-48. U.S. General Accounting Office, Washington, D. C., March 2, 1981.

Documentos Históricos. Equity of Puerto Rico, Inc., Hato Rey, P.R. 1974.

Grupo de Investigadores Puertorriqueños. *Breakthrough from Colonialism: An Interdisciplinary Study of Statehood*. Vol. I and II, Editorial de la Universidad de Puerto Rico, Río Piedras, Puerto Rico, 1984.

Leyes Fundamentales de Puerto Rico. Editorial Edil, Inc., Río Piedras, Puerto Rico, 1973.

Morales Carrión, Arturo (ed). *Puerto Rico: A Political and Cultura History*. Norton and Company, Boston, Massachusetts, 1983.

Office of the Commonwealth of Puerto Rico. *Documents on the Constitutional History of Puerto Rico*. Washington, D.C. 1944. (available in English and Spanish)

Perusse, Roland I. *et al*. *Castro's Puerto Rican Obsession*. The Cuban-American National Foundation, Washington, D.C. 1987.

_____ (ed.). *Las Relaciones entre los Estados Unidos y Puerto Rico: Documentos Básicos*. Editorial Instituto Interamericano, Hato Rey, Puerto Rico, second edition, 1987.

Quiñones Calderón, Antonio. *El Status Nuestro de Cada Día*. Ediciones Nuevas de Puerto Rico, 1984.

Ramos de Santiago, Carmen. *El Desarrollo Constitucional de Puerto Rico*. Editorial Universitaria, Universidad de Puerto Rico, Río Piedras, Puerto Rico, 1979.

_____ . *El Gobierno de Puerto Rico*. Editorial Universitaria, Universidad de Puerto Rico, Río Piedras, Puerto Rico, 1976.

Romero Barceló, Carlos. *La Estadidad es para los Pobres*. (available in English and Spanish).

_____ . "Puerto Rico, U.S.A.: The Case of Statehood," article in *Foreign Affairs*, Fall 1980, No. 59103.

Tansill, William. "The Resident Commissioner to the United States from Puerto Rico," article, U.S. Library of Congress, Washington, D.C. (undated)

Torruella, Juan R. *The Supreme Court and Puerto Rico: The Doctrine of Separate and Unequal*. Editorial de la Universidad de Puerto Rico, Río Piedras, Puerto Rico, 1985.

Smith, Carlos J. *El Status Político de Puerto Rico - Una revisión Interpretativa*. Universidad de Puerto Rico, Colegio Universitario de Cayey, Cayey, Puerto Rico, 1975.

U.S.-Puerto Rican Commission on the Status of Puerto Rico. *Status of Puerto Rico - Report*. U.S. Government Printing Office, Washington, D.C. August 1966 (in Spanish and English), reprinted by Arno Press, New York, 1975.

_____ . *Status of Puerto Rico: Selected Background Studies*. U.S. Government Printing Office, Washington, D.C., August 1966 (available in Spanish and English), reprinted by Arno Press, New York, 1975.

INDEX

A

B

Grenada, 24, 45, 51, 120, 131
    position of Severo Colberg on, 51
    position of Rubén Berríos on, 120
Grito de Lares, 16

H

H.B. 11200,   2, 36, 42, 59, 151, 152
    See also, "New Pact," "Pact of
      Permanent Union"
H.J.R. 22,   36
H.R. 23,   43, 99
H.R. 5926,   36
    See also, "Fernos-Murray bill"
Haiti, 46, 137
Hart, Gary, 38
Hawaii, 108
Hayakawa, S.I., 84
Hernández Agosto, Miguel 53-54
    position on plebiscite, 53
    position on constitutional
      convention, 53
    position on exemption from
      U.S. tariffs, 53
    position on exemption from
      U.S. maritime law, 53
    position on regulation of
      communications media, 53
    position on environmental
      control, 54
    position on control of im-
      migration, 54
    position on presidential
      primaries, 54
    position on common defense, 54
    position on language, 55
Hernández Colón, Rafael, 36, 40-57, 112, 133, 169, 170, 171
    position on UNESCO, 42, 50, 51
    position on the application
      of federal law, 42

Japan, 7, 39, 60-61, 93
    treaty with, 39, 60-61
Jarabo, José "Rony," 55, 57
    position on territorial waters, 57
    position on wild life sanctuary, 57
    position on federal regulations, 57
    position on presidential vote, 57
    position on language, 57
Javits, Jacob K., 109-110
Jones Act, 3, 10, 149
    See also, "Citizenship," "Commerce"
Jurisdiction, 7, 41
    over Caribbean National Forest, 55

K

Kemp, Jack, 105-106
Kennedy, John F., 2
Kennedy, Ted, 59
Koroma, Abdul, 135
Kozak, Michael G., 61

L

La Asamblea Constituyente, 125
Lagomarsino, Robert J., 59, 106
Language, 17-18, 108-110
    position of Colberg, 51
    position of Corrada, 84
    position of Hernández Agosto, 55
    position of Hernández Colón, 55
    position of Jackson, H., 109
    position of Jarabo, 57
    position of Javits, 109-110
    position of Muñoz, V., 56
    position of Peña Clos, 55
    position of Romero, 89
Latinamericanization, 121
    of Puerto Rican independence, 121-123, 130-131
League of Nations, 143
Liberation Movement, 30

Lopez, Jimmy, 84
Lugo Bougal, Héctor, 134

M

Macheteros, 29-32, 126, 128
    See also, "Boricua Popular Army"
Mansur, Manase, 106
Mari Bras, Juan, 125-127, 138
    position on constituent assembly, 127, 185
    position on revolution, 126
    position on statehood, 126
Martín, Fernando, 118, 124
Matsunaga, Spark M., 104
Meese, Edwin, 31
Mexico, 30
Micronesian Compact of Free Association, 79
    See also "Compact of Free Association
      between the United States and the
      Federated States of Micronesia and
      the Marshall Islands"
Migration, 9, 19-20
Military service, 6
Minimum wage, 10-11, 73, 90
Miranda, Miguel, 95
    position on presidential vote, 95
Mondale, Walter, 38
Morales, William, 30
Movement of Non-aligned Nations, 122
Muñoz Marín, Luis, 2, 35, 39, 42
Muñoz, Victoria, 55, 56-57
    position on Caribbean National Forest, 56
    position on common defense, 56
    position on independence, 56
    position on language, 56
    position on nuclear arms, 56
    position on presidential vote, 56
    position on U.S. District Court, 56
    position on U.S. maritime law, 56
    position on Voice of America, 56

Treaty of Tlatelolco, 25, 41, 56, 84, 121, 128, 130, 132
  See also "Treaty for the Prohibition
    of Nuclear Arms in Latin America"
Tutweiler, Margaret DeB., 61
Twin plants, 7, 12, 46, 61
  See also "Complementary production"

U

Udall, Morris, 93
UNCTAD, 39, 42
Unemployment, 10
UNESCO, 39, 42, 48, 50, 89
UNGA Resolution 742 (VIII), 62, 149, 151, 152
UNGA Resolution 748 (VIII), 106, 149, 150, 151
UNGA Resolution 1541 (XV), 62, 63, 151, 152
United Arab Republic, 66, 147
United Forces in Rapid Action, 28
  See also "FURA"
United Nations, 50, 88, 106, 125, 129, 130, 134, 135,
        143, 150, 152
  Decolonization Committee, 2, 43, 50, 88, 123, 129, 130,
132, 136
  General Assembly, 3, 4, 50, 121, 122, 129, 134, 135, 150
  Resolutions, 6, 130
United States Army School of the
    Americas, 127
United States Coast Guard, 26-27, 28
United States Congress, 3, 4, 5, 152
United States Constitution, 3
United States Customs Service, 9, 28
United States Department of State, 60-61, 92, 94, 129
United States District Court, 7, 17
  acceptance by NPP, 73
  bazooka attack on, 31
  Colberg position on, 48, 49
  Peña Clos position on, 55
United States Drug Enforcement
    Administration, 28

W

X, Y, Z

About the Author

Roland I. Perusse has a PhD degree in International Relations from the American University, Washington, D.C., and has held high positions in both the United States and Puerto Rican Governments. He teaches U.S.-Puerto Rican relations at the Inter American University of Puerto Rico and is Director of the Inter American Institute of Puerto Rico, a private research organization specializing in Puerto Rican affairs. After a distinguished career in the U.S. Foreign Service, he became Special Assistant for federal affairs to the Governor of Puerto Rico. He is editor of the widely-used reference volume, *Relaciones entre los Estados Unidos y Puerto Rico: Documentos Básicos*.

BOOKS OF RELATED INTEREST

Diplomatic Claims: Latin American Historians View the United States
—EDITED BY AND TRANSLATED BY WARREN DEAN

Grenada: The Untold Story
—BY GREGORY W. SANFORD AND RICHARD VIGILANTE

Haiti—Today and Tomorrow: An Interdisciplinary Study
—EDITED BY CHARLES R. FOSTER AND ALBERT VALDMAN

Jamaica: Managing Political and Economic Change
—BY JOHN D. FORBES
Co-published with the American Enterprise Institute

Mexico: Chaos on Our Doorstep
—BY SOL SANDERS

Underdevelopment Is a State of Mind: The Latin American Case
—BY LAWRENCE E. HARRISON
Co-published with the Center for International Affairs, Harvard University

Rift and Revolution: The Central American Inbroglio
—EDITED BY HOWARD J. WIARDA
Co-published by the American Enterprise Institute

The Continuing Crisis: U.S. Policy in Central America and the Caribbean
—EDITED BY MARK FALCOFF AND ROBERT ROYAL
Co-published with the Ethics and Public Policy Center

Perspectives on Pentacostalism: Case Studies from the Caribbean and Latin America
—EDITED BY STEPHEN D. GLAZIER

Small Countries, Large Issues: Studies in U.S.-Latin American Asymmetri
—BY MARK FALCOFF
Co-published with the American Enterprise Institute

Central America and the Reagan Doctrine
—EDITED BY WALTER F. HAHN

0-8191-6658-8